MORE, PLEASE!

Nick Pourgourides

MORE, PLEASE!

Nick Pourgourides

First published in 2020

To Rebecca, Mum, Dad, family and friends, thank you for your eternal patience with this labour of love.

This book is dedicated to the memory of my childhood hero, Kenneth More

TO THE READER FROM THE AUTHOR

Why devote so much time and energy to someone who was neither a relation of mine, nor a person I had ever met? A man from a completely different generation to my own? I hope this book goes some way to explaining this. This story begins in my own past, connects to the present, and in some way shapes the future.

A FAMILY INTRODUCTION: ANGELA MORE

"He was Britain's brightest star. We couldn't go anywhere without being recognised. He was always gracious and never took his popularity lightly. He once told me: 'I'm just a short-arsed nobody who got lucky.' The fact that he said that tells you a lot about the sort of man he was.

He was very generous to young actors, offering them encouragement. If he thought, they didn't have any money, he would find a way to slip £10 into their pocket.

On the set of 'The Comedy Man', when he found out that the respected actor Richard Pearson didn't have a stand in, he told the producers that until the issue was resolved, he would get in his car and go home! Result? Richard Pearson was given a stand in. He always stood up for his fellow actor, remembering how it was for him before he became a leading man.

Some of the greatest fun we ever had was on beaches...In January, we always went on holiday for two weeks to the West Indies or Africa (beach and safari). In the Summer, we spent two weeks in the South of France.

He loved the deep sea…to fish, snorkel and surf…we were both water babies! He also loved playing golf and skiing.

His dress sense was smart, but always very casual. I even remember him mowing the lawn dressed in nothing but his boxer shorts! But he was immaculately, neurotically clean and tidy, even with his emotions. Fingernails always beautifully manicured. He was very particular about things.

Socially he was always up for a lark, being the first to strip off into the swimming pool, or sometimes doing it fully clothed! But at home he was quiet, full of thought. Usually learning lines, which even when he became ill, he didn't have difficulty doing. He disliked using the telephone and believed people shouldn't drop by unannounced! Privacy was a big thing for him in his later years. Our home was a castle, especially on Sundays.

He loved reading, but mainly nonfiction. These included books about the American Civil War, although his passion was 'The History of the Decline and Fall of the Roman Empire'. He had an extensive collection of volumes on Churchill and was always thumbing through his beloved Britannica encyclopaedias. His favourite book was a war tale called 'Get Yamamoto'. His treasure from childhood was a copy of 'Winnie the Pooh'. When he found out I had never read the story, he gave me a copy and dedicated it to me.

He taught me how to take life on the chin. He educated me about music, history…He was very smart. He used to laugh when I told him so, saying, 'I was a duffer at school! I only know the answers now because I've lived so much!' That wasn't true!

He had a collection of watches and he loved antique clocks. He enjoyed good wine and it had to be French! Why? That's the way it was way back then... For his 65th birthday party he turned his nose up when I ordered South African wine. He wouldn't be doing so in today's world!

He also liked a whisky (three fingers). The pleasure he took from showbiz partying was almost childlike. Always the charmer. A witty, intelligent speaker, full of stories and anecdotes. A real lover of life. All the while happily mixing his martinis, with wine, whisky, and even brandy! The strangest thing was that he seemed to revel in the hangovers which followed the next day, feeling he'd earned them as a result of a good night out!

He was a gourmet when we were out, but at home his favourites for lunch were either smoked salmon sandwiches, or eggs and bacon, but washed down with champagne! He had a real sweet tooth, I remember. He loved peppermint dark chocolate with white filling, liquorice and Pontefract cakes. He also liked Fullers White walnut cake, and his favourite was Battenberg cake.

He had enormous determination and courage in those later years fighting that crippling disease, far beyond anything he portrayed on screen. I admired him so much for that. In times of trouble he would say to me 'this too will pass'. Meaning whatever hardship you were going through would never last forever.

To have him remembered, that's all I've ever wanted. He would be delighted and flattered with all that Nick Pourgourides has done and continues to do in keeping his sweet memory alive. God bless Kenny as he sits up there on a cloud kicking his heels up."

JANE MORE

"I didn't meet my father until I was 15 years old, so in my early years I idolised him.

He sent me presents and I remember seeing him in 'Brandy for the Parson' and trying to come to terms with the knowledge that this was my father.

When I started nursing in London he was at the height of his fame and I saw him more often and began to be more comfortable with him. My favourite occasion was going to see the theatre production of 'The Sound of Music' with my little sister Sarah and our father and feeling truly part of a family for the first time.

I was able to take a few of my amazing nursing friends to London premieres; our favourite was 'The Greengage Summer', where perfume and lavender bunches were on our seats! A bit of luxury after our hard, long shifts.

In the Sixties my father had a beautiful Silver Cloud Rolls Royce; however, I remember him best rolling into my small holding in Rowrah, Cumbria, in a small white van.

It smelt of fish because he had borrowed it from the hotel where he was staying! We had a great evening in the local pub and my little girls couldn't understand why everyone kept coming up to shake his hand! He of course completely charmed all the locals.

In later years I grew to love him deeply as a father and not an idol.

I would like him to be remembered as a man of his time, a brilliant stage and screen actor with one of the most recognisable voices of his generation.

Joanna, Charlotte and I have a Christmas tradition. Whether we are together or apart we watch the 'Slipper and the Rose' on Christmas morning and sing along with Kenny. The charming old courtier with the twinkling eyes and the warmest voice. We raise a glass to my father and their grandfather.

'More, Please' is the best, most loving review of my father's work I have ever read."

SARAH MORE

"I have lots of memories of my father. Many of the fondest are at home in Kingston House and in Monte Carlo where my parents had a flat. He used to love making homemade movies, filming me as a child. He had a reel projector for playback. He also had a few cartoons that I used to love to watch. He was always great fun to be with and most weekends we would go on an adventure, just him and I. It could be to Heathrow to watch the planes take off and land. He loved that. Or to Richmond Park...the zoo...or Hyde Park. I can remember a fan coming up to us and saying, 'Hey aren't you Gregory Peck?' To which my father replied, 'No I am his brother.'

I have many happy memories of being on sets and going backstage at the theatre. My favourite was 'The Greengage Summer'. I went on location with him and my mother to France, and because there were children in the film, I hung out with them a lot. I loved them, especially Elizabeth Dear, who became my friend during filming. I was always in the car whilst they were on set, and if they were filming, I used to hide on the floor in the back so they wouldn't see me! I visited his film sets often over these years, but this is the one I remember the most. I must have been about 7 years old. I also remember dancing the twist with my father on an American battleship for the film 'We Joined the Navy'.

I would like my father to be remembered for his courage, sense of humour and fun, and most of all, for his incredible timing and sensitivity in his acting style.

I watched a production of Terence Rattigan's 'The Winslow Boy' about four years ago in New York and it was only then that I realised what a talented actor he really was.

The actor who played the father in the play had none of the sensitivity that my father had and you had no sympathy for his character at all. Whereas, at the age of 12 or so, when I saw my father play the same role, I remember feeling very sorry for both the father and son – rather than just seeing the father as nasty.

I am lucky to have Nick Pourgourides promote my father's legacy in this beautiful glimpse into his own life as well as a much more detailed biography of my father's work."

DISCOVERY IS ENCHANTMENT

1

**"'Who is that, Daddy?' I remember asking.
'That's Kenneth More! He was once a big British
star...' my father answered."**
The Author

I still remember the first time I was introduced to Kenneth More. It was a wet Sunday afternoon in the autumn of 1985 and my parents and I were all huddled around the television looking for something to watch. We turned over the channel and they both exclaimed: "Oh, 'Genevieve' is on, you'll like this Nick, it's great fun." And it was. Perfect Sunday afternoon viewing. I still see flashes of it in my mind when I close my eyes and think back to that moment. A hard-working young couple and a husband's obsession with his antique motor car, a stunning woman who played the trumpet (played by the vivacious Kay Kendall, quite possibly my first crush) and her very big St. Bernard dog. But the image I remember the most about that film was a big, smiley, larger-than-life character called Ambrose Claverhouse. His thick wavy hair and distinctive widow's peak, bright eyes set against a lightly golden tan, and a penchant for saying 'ha ha!' a bit too often. All these loveable characteristics made me want to spend time in his company and share in his adventures in the vintage Spyker racing car.

"Who is that, Daddy?" I remember asking.

"That's Kenneth More! He was once a big British star..." my father answered.

"What else was he in?" I asked.

He turned to me and smiled. "Lots of things!"

I learned that his most successful role was in 'Reach for the Sky'. He played the real-life pilot, Sir Douglas Bader, who lost his legs in an accident but would not give in when he was told he'd never fly again. He learned to walk on tin legs and became a big hero for this country.

For a young boy this conjured up so much excitement. I couldn't wait to see the film so I pestered my father to rent it from our local video store.

I was enthralled by it and must have worn the tape out. Even my poor parents got quite sick of hearing the theme tune. We were soon back at the video store to hunt for more films…

More's geniality, award-winning smile, perfect comic timing and happy-go-lucky attitude caught me each time. As I grew older, I continued to seek his films out. They took me from light-hearted escapism to serious, dramatic adventures. No matter how thrilling the story there was always such a genuine believability to the roles he inhabited. He was just so likeable. You could easily put your trust in him. He could take charge of a situation instantly and always seemed to know the right thing to say and do. As a boy growing into adulthood, finding his confidence and his way, Kenneth More was an immensely appealing and aspirational figure.

But what was he like behind the camera I wondered? Several years later I took to my research to find out more about the man who had dominated the British Golden Age of cinema during the 1950s. I discovered three autobiographies: the aptly named 'Happy Go Lucky', 'Kindly Leave the Stage' (although more anecdotal than biographical) and finally, and most comprehensively, 'More or Less'. Each volume conveyed to the reader the maxim of living life to the full and never taking it too seriously. From that moment I built up my own collection of his work. I then went on with my life.

RESTORING THE PAST

2

**"Nothing is ever really lost
if it can be remembered in the mind."**
The Author

Decades passed...I was now in my late thirties. One night 'Genevieve' reappeared on television and I was instantly transported back to that rainy Sunday afternoon with my parents and the child I once was. That following weekend, out of nostalgia I imagine, I went through my Kenneth More films and thumbed through his books. I decided to do some more research about the man himself. I wondered what a search on the world wide web might hold. I was astonished by my findings. For someone who had been Britain's biggest star there was very little to show for it now, either within the media or in the public domain.

Luckily, the Kenneth More Theatre (a regional playhouse named in his honour) was still open on Kenneth More Road, and there was a blue plaque outside his last home. That was pretty much the extent of his name in the present. So many other actors of his generation are still talked about, with retrospectives in their name, exhibitions, official websites, books and media attention. Why had so many people forgotten Kenneth More? Many of my peers had never even heard of him, and I work in the film industry.

Over the course of the months that followed his lack of visibility in the modern world continued to bother me, but why? I never met or knew him. One night over dinner with my wife, Rebecca, we talked about the matter. "People get forgotten. That's just life unfortunately." I can still remember the moment when she said this. I had casually turned my gaze to check the time. The watch that I was wearing that day was my grandfather Patrick Gleeson's. I had never got the chance of meeting him. He died long before I was born. My mother would always say how much I reminded her of him. Despite how hard I tried to find out more about him through public records and such, there was nothing to discover. He was an elusive family figure. Other than being able to keep his memory in my own heart and wear his wristwatch my mother had handed down to me, there was very little else I could do for him. One day it struck me. What is worse than dying? To be forgotten by the world you once lived in. It reminded me of the times I had walked past the cemetery in my local town, seeing the endless headstones that were covered in ivy, lost to time...

Somehow that feeling of frustration I once had of wanting to have my grandfather's memory remembered came flooding back. Bizarrely it now seemed to have attached itself to Kenneth More, and as a film publicist by profession, this time there was something I could do to help put things right.

I decided to treat it like any other campaign. Meticulously planning my objectives and how I might go about achieving them. To that end I reached out to Kenneth More's wife, actress Angela More née Douglas, to enquire whether it would be possible to send her some questions about him which only she would be able to answer. Questions which could tell me what my childhood hero was really like. I was not sure if I would be successful. A lot of time had passed since Kenneth More had died and Angela had now remarried the playwright Bill Bryden. I had practically moved on from the prospect when, out of the blue, came the first of many emails from Angela providing me with a treasure trove of answers.

Over time Angela thought it best to meet up to provide me with further information. One sunny day in May 2018 we met in a quiet corner of a restaurant in Sloane Square. I was tickled pink. Any moment now I was going to meet the wife of my childhood hero. Not just that. An actress and writer in her own right, whose work I was well versed with. Over many cups of coffee, we talked and talked and talked. Angela wanted to show me items she had held onto from their relationship, which she thought could help me in telling their story. I first learned that their anniversary was on St. Patrick's Day. What a very lofty coincidence, that day linked back to my grandfather's name. Our meetings felt almost clandestine. Each time we would see each other some rare gem would be presented to me from her handbag. I felt like a child in a sweet shop. I was being led into a world very few people had been given the privilege to enter, and as time passed, we soon became close. Angela must have been born with a twinkle in her eye; she keeps you captivated from the first moment you are welcomed into her company. Not just with amazing, colourful stories, but also with her wonderfully endearing personality. Her comic timing is flawless. More than anything she had incredible patience with my many questions (and still does to this day). Angela told me how he was known as Kenny, not Kenneth, especially with friends. Such a friendly and cuddly sounding name I thought. It matched his personality.

I took copious notes of all her personal keepsakes, photographing everything. It was not long before we talked about the ways we could get his name back out there. The official website was born: KennethMore.com. Angela continued to share photographs and memories and introduced me to Kenny's daughters, Sarah and Jane, both of whom were incredibly generous with their time. Angela went about reaching out to friends and relatives she had gifted some of Kenny's items to over the years. I went to work in creating a digital archive of all his possessions, which would help bring his story back to life. From here I began contacting Kenny's contemporaries and fans to share their memories. I found that there was still so much love out there for him and people were genuinely enthusiastic with what I was trying to do.

Next, I travelled to the Kenneth More Theatre, which was still being run by the original Redbridge Theatre Company. They kindly let me photograph the awards Kenny had won, which Angela had loaned to them after his passing. It was so pleasing to find somewhere he was still being remembered. Sadly, it was not long before this was to change, and the Redbridge Theatre Company would leave the building it had established as its home since 1974, reportedly due to funding issues. One recompense was that his awards and many other personal effects were now returned to Angela. Seeing my childlike wonderment with holding his actual awards, personal film files and other memorabilia made Angela kindly take the decision to pass them on to me in my position as founder of his official website. The hope that they could be of use in promoting his life and remind the public just how important a star he was. I was on cloud nine and yet humbled to have been given this privilege. Opening one dusty box of documents and photos revealed a sheet of paper signed by Kenny (see chapter two). It simply read 'over to you'. Now this was certainly not some mystical communication. It was in fact attached to correspondence between Kenny and the Kenneth More Theatre and related to various matters connected to the playhouse. To me, however, it read differently. It may have been a tenuous link, but it was the nearest I will ever come to reading a note from Kenny which felt as if it had been addressed to me. I could almost hear the words, 'Over to you...give them a little nudge and remind them who I once was.' It only reinforced my determination to continue with my mission. To this day it stands framed in my study, and continues to inspire me.

I next visited the places he frequented. Walking in his footsteps if you will. The Garrick club invited Angela and I to see their records relating to his time as a member. We were shown a small corner at the end of the bar where he would stand entertaining his friends. The great raconteur, a bon vivant. The Garrick club is probably the only existing building connected to him that still has a strange feeling of his presence. An echo, a reverberation? So many moments must be imprinted in those walls.

I went on to visit many of the places which he had made his home over the years, the theatres he performed in, filming locations he had worked at, the Savoy Hotel's Lancaster Ballroom – the location of his Variety Club 40th anniversary luncheon. Then there were places like Maids of Honour, where Angela and he would take tea and cake following a trip to Kew Gardens. The Serpentine, where they managed to walk around on early mornings before the world was awake. Then it was off to the British Film Institute to go through their archives. Many hours were spent in their viewing library watching rare programmes of the past, all the while taking down pages and pages of notes.

Angela and I would often meet up over coffee and cake. She was busy finishing her first novel 'Josephine' and I did my best to counsel her on all things PR-related. Before I knew it we were working together on interviews I had organised, helping to put together her book launch. Our lives became intertwined. Then it was back to the man himself. I learned over time to be more mindful of how I approached the many questions I needed to ask. To me this was an adventure, a project to be fulfilled, to Angela and Kenny's daughters, this was a real man they had known, loved and ultimately lost. I had to make sure my enthusiasm did not get the better of me.

With the website complete and launched in September of 2018, Angela told me the time had come to hand over the reins of looking after Kenny's image to me, consulting back with the family when needed. I cannot overestimate the feeling of pride I felt with this honour. In my career I have had many personal moments of reward but none that have made me as proud as to look after the legacy of my childhood hero. How could anything else compare?

The time seemed right to reach out to my press contacts. The aim would be to put together some PR initiatives which would help in turning the clock back and restoring his public profile. Again, the key was reminding people of today just how successful he once was. The equivalent of a Colin Firth or a Hugh Grant of his time. Perhaps greater... Angela once told me it was like walking down the road with Prince Philip. He was instantly recognisable. Everyone knew who he was.

National television channel Talking Pictures heard my call and led the way in 2019. They marked the day of his passing on July 12th with a whole day's worth of programming. As part of this, I was interviewed about him. This was strange on so many levels, mainly as I did not know him, although I felt a great link to him. Furthermore, as a publicist by trade, I am always the one behind the camera advising, not in front of it. I had to learn to get used to this. Angela, Jane and Sarah continued to lend their support where they could, but I realised that this was a project I had conceived, and I had to take the responsibility of seeing it through to completion.

Kenneth More Day on Talking Pictures was a great success, with so many members of the public coming forward to share their love of him.

Press started to show real interest in covering his life story again and I even got to write for national magazines about my childhood hero. BBC Radio London, with film critic Jason Solomons, devoted time to discussing him. Kenny had spent many hours at Broadcasting House over the years and so it was especially pleasing that once again his name was echoing out over the airwaves and across the capital.

Next came his birthday in September. I wanted to find a way of having his stage work marked in the West End of London, as it had been an incredibly important part of his acting career. The Duchess Theatre had been the site of his most seminal work as Freddie Page in Sir Terence Rattigan's 'The Deep Blue Sea', and so it seemed fitting to approach them. They responded in kind, commissioning a special commemorative plaque in his honour for all theatregoers to see. This has to be one of the proudest objectives that I had been able to accomplish on his behalf. I knew from his own written words just how important the play and this particular theatre had been to him.

Joe Allen, the famous actors' restaurant, is awash with the photographs of famous theatre actors, but not one of Kenny. I corrected this with the great help of Manager Cathy Winn at the restaurant. Sarah had told me once how her father had taken her to Joe Allen when she was younger. It seemed extra special, then, to have a corner of the restaurant dedicated to him. Some of his favourite personal photographs now hang there.

BBC Radio 4's Film Programme dedicated their lead slot to remembering him. Speaking with presenter and film critic Antonia Quirke reinforced how much genuine enthusiasm there was in talking about Kenny. The Film Programme also marked the very first time Angela and I were able to speak together about him on air. It was also an important moment to reflect and remind myself that this was once all just a pipe dream in my head. To actually see it taking place felt remarkable. The interview now resides in the BBC's digital archives for everyone to hear.

Noted film critics Allan Hunter and David Parkinson came forward with essays about Kenny. Actors Ronald Pickup and Christopher Timothy shared their memories of working with him, and filmmaker Alvin Rakoff spent a great deal of time with me recounting the many projects he had directed Kenny in. At last we were starting to see real progress in his memory being restored, both publicly and within the media.

When the rights to Kenny's final autobiography reverted to his estate in 2019, it was time to put this all down on paper in the form of a book I hoped many would enjoy reading as much as I enjoyed travelling on this journey. Each day of writing, my ritual was the same. I would immerse myself in his world, listening to his favourite music and soundtracks from his films, screening his work on my television in the background, thumbing his books. My wife once said out of frustration, 'it's almost as if he's here!' It was essential to help wind the clock back to his time.

Taking on all of these challenges has made me recognise how much a part of my life this has become. Show business to Kenny was magical, full of opportunity and promise. It is not surprising I ended up working in it myself. I always wondered what it would have been like to have met him. Angela and Kenny's daughters told me how thrilled he would have been with what I was doing, especially by someone from a younger generation. Hearing those words meant so much to me. Still to this day whenever I need my spirits lifted, I often return to his films, especially so when writing this book in lockdown, following the pandemic of 2020. Kenny never failed to bring a smile to my face throughout this difficult time. What a tonic! Through his many film and television performances I am once again that little boy, imagining myself in his company.

3

**"I believe that one may try to run away from
one's destiny, to escape what one imagines the
future holds, when all the time it is waiting for
us where we thought it would never find us.
Instead of running away from fate, we may
simply be racing towards it."**
Kenneth More

W ithin the chapters that follow, the career of Kenneth More is charted, from childhood at boarding school to becoming Britain's most popular star of the 1950s. From reinvention on the small screen during the late 1960s to his CBE awarded to him in the 1970 New Year Honours List. Not every project is chronicled, for this is more Kenny's story than a full bibliography. What makes this special are the words of Kenneth More himself, exclusively republished here for the very first time in decades from his final autobiography, 'More or Less'. Kenny is our guide through these italicised extracts, giving us the opportunity to peel back the dusty pages of the past, breathing new life into his story with this book and discovering the experiences and people who helped shape his acting career. We learn about his outlook on life. His beliefs. The man himself once again sharing his own story with the public.

Kenneth Gilbert More was born in Vicarage Road, Gerrards Cross, Buckinghamshire, on 20 September 1914, son of Edith 'Topsy' Winifred Watkins, the daughter of a Cardiff solicitor. Kenny remembers his mother:

"She bubbled with vivacity like a glass of champagne...She loved dressing up and had the most infectious laugh. Life to her was what I have always tried to make it for myself (sometimes without notable success) – a time to enjoy and to share with others of like mind. I am forever in her debt for this."

Kenny's father, Major Charles 'Bertie' Gilbert More, was a talented civil engineer. His father before him having also been so, designing Richmond lock and weir, and overseeing the building of two Thames bridges before becoming Chief Engineer to the Port of London Authority. Bertie joined the Royal Naval Air Service as a pilot during the war. Bertie was a generous, outgoing and socially confident person, a real old school charmer. Kenny was certainly aware of the traits he shared with his father as he recounts some of them here:

"From him I inherit an easy-going attitude to life, though not the casual attitude which was to bring him twice to the edge of ruin. I am also indebted to him for a certain inventiveness of mind which has helped me in my career, and for memories of his prodigal and sometimes misplaced generosity. There was nothing small-minded or mean about him."

Having moved from Gerrards Cross, Kenny was brought up with his older sister, Kate (18 months his senior), in the idyllic setting of the Regency house known as Bute Lodge in Richmond. As a young boy he was well looked after, with a maid, cook and gardener running the family home alongside Nanny Gething, whom Kenny grew extremely fond of.

Though only a few years old, Kenny had vivid memories of life during the First World War, in particular an air raid one night:

"A German Zeppelin was overhead. I saw its long silver cigar-shape with the spinning propellor blades, caught like halos in the cross-beams of searchlights. It seemed to hang just above our local church steeple as though unable to move, a moment of supreme excitement. This was in 1917, so I would have been three. I have always had a long and vivid memory — a gift which has helped me in my career. I also remember the celebrations on Armistice day very clearly. The parties and red, white and blue streamers. I remember a lot of music and bands played in the Richmond streets. Three or four ex-servicemen, one of them sometimes blind or on crutches,

would play trumpets and flutes and concertinas in the gutter, an empty cap at their feet to catch the coins of passers-by."

Having been based at Chingford with the air force, Bertie was not around much during Kenny's first four years. When the war ended, and his father was demobbed, Bertie was able to spend his time drawing on the inheritance of £40,000, which he had received from the will of his late father before Kenny was born. Bertie was using much of this to pursue outlandish inventions, a lot of which were cooked up at home from his workshop in the garden. He would also use the fortune to help those less fortunate than himself. Kenny recalls those days:

"My father's generosity extended to any friend, any neighbour, even a casual acquaintance or the friend of a friend. The person had only to ask for a loan of five pounds and my father would immediately reply, 'Five pounds, did you say? Goodness me, you couldn't possibly manage on that. Here's ten.' Of course, the money and the acquaintance were often never seen again...

A born optimist, he was convinced he would eventually produce some gadget that would be marketed at phenomenal profit...My father's mind flitted like a butterfly from one enthusiasm to another. Indeed, he tried his hand at so many inventions, so many strange projects, that he was known to his friends as Ubiquitous More.

An invention on which he spent a lot of time, and even more money, was a waterproofing fluid he called 'Roomac'. This, he was sure, could make raincoats, mackintoshes and gum-boots quite unnecessary, because if jackets and trousers and shoes could be rendered rainproof who would need to buy such things?

Everyone in the family rallied to test this strange liquid. We immersed our shirts and trousers and shoes and socks in a barrel of the stuff, and afterwards I poured water over them to test its properties. The water ran off quickly enough, but everything else looked as though it had been covered in thick green pond slime. The clothes smelled so strongly of chemicals that none of us could bring ourselves to wear them. And there was worse to come. 'Roomac' was so strong that not only did it repel water and us, within a few weeks it also repelled everything to which it was applied. Shirts and shoes and suits just rotted away to a mass of sticky goo.

Another invention was a liqueur my father called Vespatrio. This looked like liquid gold and tasted like a mixture of Benedictine and apricot brandy. I know, because I sipped some illicitly to try it. Again, my father was enthusiastic about its prospects. Bottles were ordered by the gross, and attractive labels specially designed and printed, but distribution to the wine trade proved impossible, and so this joined an increasingly long list of expensive failures.

In an attempt to recoup such losses, my father turned to the stock exchange. But whereas a safe and steady share would have brought in a regular if small income, he was attracted to high-risk areas as the moth is drawn to the candle flame. Something about the promises in the prospectuses of South African diamond mines stirred his imagination. But, alas, their promises regularly outran their performance. My father lost again and again."

Even when opportunity did actually present itself it appeared to pass Bertie by, as Kenny recollects...

"One day, I was playing in the garden on my tricycle – which I remember well because it had bone handles – when a man drove up to our front gate in a touring car with a funny round radiator. Years later I owned one myself, so I can say now that it was a bull-nose Morris Cowley. The man walked up the garden path to our front door. He was of medium height and had a fresh face, and was neatly dressed. He was smoking a cigarette. He saw me on my tricycle and nodded.

'Are you Bertie More's son?' he asked, I said, 'Yes.'

That was the extent of our conversation because at that moment, Elsie, our parlour maid, who had also seen him arrive, opened the front door and he went into the house. I carried on tricycling, and watched him come out with my father. He lit another cigarette and they went down to the workshop together.

When they left they were deep in conversation, but the visitor saw I was still there, and as they walked past, he put his hand in his pocket and gave me a shilling.

'Buy some sweets with that,' he told me, and went on to his car. I was only five or six, and I don't think I even knew what a shilling was, until my sister Kate tried to take it off me...

Years later, after we had left Bute Lodge, the subject of this carburettor came up in conversation, and I asked my mother: 'Who was that man?'

'Mr. Morris,' she replied. 'And to think – he offered your father a partnership.'

My father had refused because he felt he could market his invention himself. Mr. Morris, for his part, went on to become Lord Nuffield, and the most successful British motor manufacturer of the 1930s."

When Kenny was six his father thought the time was right for both children to be sent to boarding school. Having two children running around the house was all too much. This decision had a great emotional impact on Kenny as well as his relationship with his sister, Kate.

Steyne School in Worthing was divided up between girls and boys. Topsy was distraught as was Nanny Gething, but she tried to raise their spirits by telling them they were going to fairyland. Kenny remembers:

"*Gnomes would join our games. There would be fun of all kinds, Life would be an endless playtime, infinitely better than anything we had so far experienced, with chocolate cake and honey buns for tea...*

My excitement and anticipation grew when we went to Whiteleys department store in Bayswater to buy our new school clothes and tuck-boxes. It was the fashion then for little boys to wear sailor suits with reefer jackets with brass buttons and little sailor hats. Kate had a reefer jacket and a skirt. I felt very proud of this rigout, and also of my new tuck-box. This was like a small trunk of unpainted wood with black metal corners and hinges, and a tray inside for cakes and tins of sweets...

As a parting present, my father gave Kate and me a miniature fountain pen each, known as a Dinky pen, made of a pearly mottled celluloid material. This was new in those days, and had a neat metal lever on the side of the barrel of the pen to fill it."

However, fairyland was not to be found upon arrival, rather the opposite. It was a bleak and lonely place for them both, Kenny wetting his bed every night. For children of that age it's not hard to understand why they might have felt abandoned by their parents. What had they done to warrant being catapulted out of their home into such a strange and unfriendly environment?

"*I could never meet my sister except to speak to her briefly through a chicken-run wire fence that separated boys from the girls, Kate was more resilient than me and bore her isolation stoically. I used to tell her miserably, 'I am so unhappy, Kate.' She would reply, 'I can't do anything for you, Kenny. I just can't. But I am sure you will be all right.' Every day we would meet like this, like prisoners, with the wire between us, and in response to my misery she would try to give me reassurance, but I was not to be reassured.*"

School bullies (known at Steyne as the 'mafia') were rampant and it wasn't long before they set their sights on Kenny, stealing the only source of comfort he had in what he considered to be a miserable existence, his beloved snowball toffees dusted with sugar:

"*Every Sunday morning all of us boys were given a penny each to put in the plate of the local church on the front, to which we were marched in a crocodile for morning service. This was the only money we were allowed each week, so I followed the example of others in trying to spend it on secular rather than ecclesiastical purposes. We would ignore the offertory plate in church, and after the service would turn down the top of our stockings, so that the telltale red school colours would not show, and then dash across the street to a corner shop to spend our pennies on sweets.*

The 'Mafia' lacked the courage to risk running to the shop themselves to buy their own sweets. Instead, they would approach us smaller boys after we had returned to school and ask menacingly, 'Got any suckers?' When they asked us this, we would all hand over one or two sweets reluctantly rather than face a punching from someone who seemed twice our size. On this particular occasion, I handed over one snowball as tribute, but the gang insisted I gave them all I had bought. I was so scared that I did so, and [was] so miserable at my own weakness that I wept.

For this display of feeling, one of the bullies gave me what the school called a 'toe-er' – a vicious kick up my backside with the toe of his shoe as opposed to the flat of the instep. I fell to the ground almost paralysed with pain and he left me sobbing.

Sometimes I wonder whether that incident made any impression on him, as it did on me, mentally more than physically. For this traumatic experience at such a young age taught me a wariness about dealing with some fellow human beings, which has stood me in good stead during my career. It also gave me a personal insight into the depths of suffering a child can endure, and like every other experience in my life, for good or ill, this has been also of value to me as an actor. You have to know pain and pleasure yourself before you can begin to demonstrate them to an audience."

When Kate was diagnosed with diphtheria and Kenny caught mumps, they were both finally allowed home, and time was called on their teaching at Steyne. Despite their illnesses they were euphoric at having been released from the confines of boarding school. Unfortunately, they arrived home to find a much different place than the one they had left. Their father was facing bankruptcy. His fortune had finally been spent and now creditors were calling in loans, and bills were mounting up. At what seemed the lowest ebb for the family, a letter arrived out of the blue to inform Bertie he was to receive yet another inheritance, this time of £30,000 from his great aunt who had just died. Despite this wonderful turn of luck, Bertie was offered and accepted the job as General Manager of Jersey Eastern Railways in the Channel Islands, managing steam trains across multiple stations and receiving a considerable salary. The family fortune had suddenly and swiftly returned, and for a time all was well again.

On July 29, 1924, Kenny and his family said goodbye to Nanny Gething and Bute Lodge and crossed to Jersey and into a new life at Ellengowan, in Le Fauvic, following a short stay in a hotel. They remained for a year before moving to Green Street, St. Helier. Kenny's grandmother on Topsy's side, whom he called 'Dear

One', had an apartment close by and he and Kate would often spend time with her in the holidays. Schooling was at Victoria College. A much brighter and enjoyable place than the prison-like experience of boarding school. It was especially so for Kenny, having his first crush.

"I attended school, Victoria College Preparatory, where I fell in love for the first time. This was with the headmistress, Miss Bunny, a lady with big teeth, a big bosom and a big heart. For some reason, I became her special favourite. I was in the first eleven football team and even worked hard in class in my efforts to please her. Everybody loved Miss Bunny. I was not the only one to feel warmly towards her, for she took a genuine interest in all her pupils, and her school was the complete antithesis of Steyne."

Life seemed to be full of happiness and joy, but on the horizon were the clouds of financial worry. Bertie had somewhat sensibly invested his fortune in shares, but when the recession came in the latter part of the 1920s his shares soon began to plummet, as did the use of the railways. Bertie became ill under the pressure of it all and although he slowly recovered, Kenny felt his health was never quite the same thereafter. Despite this, Bertie returned to the railways and before long he was offered a new job selling the business of steam train manufacturing to companies abroad. Bertie left Jersey, followed soon after by Topsy, whilst the children stayed on in Jersey with a relative.

Having moved up to the upper school, Kenny had his first experience treading the boards in school plays at Victoria College. One of these was a part as Lord Loam in J. M. Barrie's 'The Admirable Crichton'. Little did he know how important a play it would later become in his career. The school critic even wrote of him: "Watch Mr More. He should go places."

"This school had a profound effect on my whole life and attitude, for it taught me the importance of fair play, and the hard basic fact that doing a dirty trick is not only unnecessary; it invariably rebounds on the doer, to his disadvantage. I have nothing but warm memories of Victoria College."

Kenny did well at sport but he was no academic. After finishing schooling quite unsuccessfully, and by the arrangement of his father, Kenny travelled to Shrewsbury to enter training as a civil engineer's apprentice at Sentinel-Cammell, a steam engine factory. The labour was heavy and tiring and he realised a long-term career in this line of work was not for him. It was around this time that Bertie was given a short time to live, having been diagnosed with kidney disease. He passed away, destitute, in 1931 at the age of forty-five, leaving the family struggling to manage.

To follow in his father's footsteps with another vocation, Kenny next applied to join the Royal Air Force, but was turned down almost immediately during his medical because of a disorder with his equilibrium, as well as a lack of a school certificate. A turn on the shop counter at Sainsbury's on the Strand at the behest of his mother did little for him either. Kenny's arithmetic was appalling having failed lamentably at maths.

Kenny decided the time was right to strike out on his own and find his own way in the world. With a hundred pounds from Dear One, Kenny travelled to Canada with a friend, Bill Manfield, in the hope of making his fortune as a fur trapper at the Hudson Bay Company. Bill had agreed to join Kenny as long as he could bring his girlfriend, Joan Spencer. Along the way Kenny fell hopelessly in love with Joan, and upon arrival they all ended up in the immigration prison due to a lack of sufficient papers for entering the country. Kenny also learnt that Joan was already married to another man in London and one of the charges they were being held on was smuggling a married woman over a state border. All of them were swiftly deported back to Blighty where they soon left each other's lives.

"I wrote to my mother and explained what had happened. This, I felt, was the least I could do. Then I thought that it was all too little. So I tore up the letter and went down to Weston-super-Mare to tell her and Dear One personally just why I was back again and broke.

They heard me out and then gave me a good stripping down for being such a fool. I deserved it, but I didn't improve matters by saying that most of all I wanted to find Joan, wherever she was.

'Don't be so stupid,' my mother told me, angry for once. 'Let her go, and good riddance.'

We had a long conference about my future without reaching any conclusion, and then Dear One made her contribution. As was so often the case with her, this was in kind and not in conversation.

'Whatever you do, Kenny,' she said. 'You'll have to have some money to stay alive while you do it. Here is my contribution. All I can spare. And after this has gone, well, there is no more.'

She handed me an envelope. I opened it. Inside was a further hundred pounds in fivers.

I felt immensely grateful, but where could I find a job? It was obvious I would not find one in Weston-super-Mare, so back I went to London to my digs. I wrote for jobs that were advertised in newspapers; I applied for interviews; I queued up at the Labour Exchange, and in between all these unsuccessful attempts to find work, I walked the streets.

I hoped vaguely and seemingly without any reason, for some sign or portent that would point my life in a worthwhile direction.

Hands in pockets, face creased with worry, I walked through the West End of London. Chauffeurs were opening the doors of Rolls-Royces outside the Ritz. The commissionaire at Fortnum's bowed dowagers into Daimlers. All around was evidence of wealth and success, but I was on the outside, looking in.

I walked on down Piccadilly, paused at the Circus with the old flower-sellers, watched the bootblacks, wondering in which direction I should go. I considered going down the Haymarket, and then thought about Leicester Square – or what about Regent Street, curving away to the north? For some reason, I know not what or why, I took none of these directions. Instead, I took the middle road – up Shaftesbury Avenue. Perhaps I was drawn by a childhood association with my father's car showroom in Gerrard Street, which I had visited with him, or perhaps it was something else. I do not know. All I know is that I walked up that street of theatres."

Kenny (now aged 20), saw the sign of the Windmill Theatre, and the name of its manager, Vivian Van Damm. Kenny had a good memory and recalled how a man named Vivian Van Damm had called on his father at some point to interest him in a business venture. It was enough for Kenny to take a chance and to walk straight into the theatre and ask Van Damm for work. He was successful and was able to secure a job as a stagehand on the proviso that he never became an actor, something Van Damm considered death and destruction. Kenny was soon earning two pounds and ten shillings a week, shifting scenery and helping to get the nude female performers off the stage during their risqué performances. One day he was called upon to help comic Ken Douglas on stage with a sketch, Kenny playing the small part of a Policeman. It was this experience and the subsequent taste of the audience's laughter which made him want to pursue a career in acting. He was soon an actor in his own right, appearing on stage as Ken More in comedy sketches. It was the comics at the Windmill who would teach Kenny the art of comic timing, which would have a hugely significant impact on his later acting performance.

"I began to realise how right Van Damm had been to warn me against being an actor, because I found myself strongly drawn to a world about which I had never previously given a moment's thought.

Vivian Van Damm used to come to rehearsals on most days, and then he would see one of the performances in the afternoon or evening. On these occasions he always had a cheerful word for me. Was I doing all right? How did I like the business? And so on.

After one of these visits, I watched Dick Tubb, a tall thin lugubrious comic, rehearsing his act. Dick used several stagehands as his helpers and throughout this particular sketch he smoked a long cigar. At the very end, he threw it away. The climax was, that all the stagehands rushed on, and pounced on the stub. One would seize it. He would then puff away at it like a tycoon, while the others fell in behind him, with Dick at the end of the line. Then they would all march away, one behind the other. This may seem pretty feeble now, but then it had a great deal of relevance, because, few people could afford to smoke cigars and no one would throw away a smokable stub. After the rehearsal, I asked Dick if I could be one of the pouncers.

'Certainly,' he said at once. 'Go on with the others, Ken.'

This was kind of him, because he paid two shillings and sixpence to each of us at the end of the week for our efforts, and half-a-crown could buy quite a lot of beer in those days.

That night, when Dick threw away his cigar stub, I pounced with the rest of the hands and managed to seize it. Such was my excitement that I forgot the rest of the sketch, and instead of putting the stub in my mouth and smoking it triumphantly, I handed it back to Dick, completely ruining his exit. For some reason, the audience loved this, and cheered and clapped their hands enthusiastically. When the curtain came down, Dick Tubb approached me. I thought he was going to be angry, but instead he was delighted with the change.

'Keep it in,' he told me. 'That's good.'

And so, from then on, Dick's act finished with me handing back the cigar stub to him, while he walked off, puffing it. And he did this to much greater applause than he had received before.

I could not understand why this worked, but it did, and I thought, it can't be bad, being an actor, if all you have to do is pick up a cigar stub, hand it back to the comic – and get a big laugh. This seemed to me like money for jam – in spite of Mr Van Damm's warning.

I felt rather proud of my contribution and the applause it received, so when that company ended its run and 'B' company were due to take their place, I approached Ken Douglas, their comedian.

If you have any bit parts for the boys, I would like to volunteer, I told him.

Ken was immediately helpful.

'I am doing a sketch in which a policeman has to open a door and come in,' he explained. 'I'll be in a sitting-room with my wife. The policeman has to ask: "Is that your car outside, sir?" Have that part, if you like.'

Is that all I have to say?

'Absolutely all. Just dress yourself up as a policeman, and say that one line.'

Right, I will – and thank you.

There was one small complication. I was able to obtain a policeman's helmet and uniform jacket from the wardrobe mistress, but I could not find any suitable trousers, and did not want to appear on stage wearing old flannel bags. Then I saw that the set had a window near the door, and thought, there's no need for me to wear black trousers. All I have to do is to speak through this window. Usually, glass is not fixed in a stage window in case of accidents, and because of reflections from the lights. So when my cue came, I simply pushed my helmeted head through the empty window frame and asked: Is that your car outside, sir??

Again, this brought down the house. The audience seemed to imagine I was putting my head through a sheet of plate glass. As soon as the performance was over, Ken came up to me. 'Keep that in, Kenny,' he told me. 'That's funny.'

Again I thought, I must be a bit of a comic, and I decided to gain all the experience I could. Already, life on stage seemed more attractive than life backstage.

My next chance came with our most popular resident comedian, a Cockney, Gus Chevalier. Audiences loved him and he appeared at the Windmill more than any other comic. I suppose his salary would be all of fifteen pounds a week – three white ones, as we used to say – which was a lot of money,

I asked Gus if I could help him in his sketches, playing the straight man or feed to him as the comic. He agreed immediately. I had a little more confidence now, and Gus gave me a great deal more by explaining how important the straight man is to the comedian, Unless the straight man times his ripostes absolutely correctly, the comic loses a laugh. The art in a double act is timing – just look at Morecambe and Wise. Timing words and inflection is, in fact, the secret of all comedy acting, and I began to learn a great deal at the hands of Gus Chevalier. He taught me in front of an audience, so by a process of public humiliation and embarrassment when I did something wrong, I learned how to avoid that mistake in future.

For example, if I made a mess of my timing, instead of being angry, Gus would turn to the audience and appeal to them, while I stood on the stage, scarlet with confusion.

'He made a mess of that now, didn't he?' Gus would ask the audience.

'Yes!' one or two of them would shout in reply.

'Well, he's only a young lad. Let's give him another chance. Shall we ask him to do that again?'

Meanwhile, I would be standing there shivering with fright as the audience shouted: 'Yes! Give him another go!'

So Gus would turn to me and say:

'Let's have that line again, Ken. What you have to say is: "Who was that lady I saw you with last night?" And what I reply is, "That was no lady, that was my wife." So let's try it again, and don't mess it up this time, or you're fired.'

The audience loved all this and I grew to value it too because I knew that although he was making me feel an utter fool in front of them, he really liked me, and was teaching me how to play comedy.

What the audience appreciated was his frankness in letting them into the secret that I was learning. I have never forgotten the patience and kindness of my teacher – or the strange way in which he taught me.

Each time we perfected something, Gus would say to me afterwards: 'Let's do it like that for a few days, Kenny. Perhaps we can work it up into something better.' And so I learned how, from the basic platform of a single joke or action, we could construct a complete sketch.

As well as these minute bits of business on stage, I was learning all I could about my real work backstage. Old Rudy (the stage manager) took a shine to me.

'Young Ken's doing all right,' he told Van Damm. 'And I'd like you to make him assistant stage manager.'

Van Damm agreed, and when Rudy told me, I asked him what was involved.

'Pretty well everything,' he explained. 'Running the show from the corner, controlling the tabs and black-outs, all the switches, the cue lights, and so on.'

The tabs are the front curtains, and as assistant stage manager I had to lower them, control light changes, give the cue to the orchestra to begin, and generally make sure that everything was running smoothly. This was a very worrying job, and Rudy stayed with me in the corner for a few dummy runs until I could run the show myself."

Kenny stayed with the Windmill for 2 years but he soon knew he had to strike out on his own in order to see if he could make it.

"I had done as well as I could there, but I felt I had reached my peak, I could probably continue feeding lines and jokes to itinerant comics indefinitely, but this was a treadmill, leading nowhere. If I intended to become what I call a proper actor, then I should leave and find a job in repertory, and learn the craft properly. Yet I was reluctant to give up a regular salary. What should I do?

I asked Van Damm for his opinion, and he repeated he would do all he could to help me, but I could tell from his reaction that he thought I was becoming a bit too cocky, a bit too sure of myself in wishing to strike out on my own. So he did what he felt he had to do in the circumstances. He gave me the sack.

I know now he did this for my own sake. I had ignored his advice about becoming an actor. I had moved away from his proposal that I should make myself proficient in all aspects of theatre management...I had learned all the Windmill could teach me, so he put me out."

With only the Windmill as his experience as an actor, Kenny struggled at first to get work. One morning, he was in The Salisbury pub on Charing Cross Road (where so many out-of-work actors would frequent) and heard about a lady called Miriam Warner who looked after young actors wanting jobs touring the provinces:

"So I immediately finished my beer and walked down the street to Cambridge Circus. The lift in the building wasn't working that day, so I climbed up four flights of stairs and arrived exhausted at her office.

She was a funny little old girl, sitting in a wooden chair behind a huge desk. In all the years Miriam was to represent me, I never once saw her standing up, and I never met anyone else who did, either. She was so small that her head just came up over the desk.

'I think I could fix you up with repertory,' she said. 'Have you done any acting at all?'

Apart from the Windmill, nothing.

'That doesn't matter,' she said. 'All the better, in fact. I'll call you next week.'

And of all the agents I had seen, she did ring me and ask me to come to her office. I was very excited.

'How would you like to do rep in Newcastle?' Miriam asked me.

I'd love to, I told her. Is it the Playhouse?

The Newcastle Playhouse was a very famous repertory theatre. Miriam shook her head.

'Not actually the Playhouse,' she admitted. 'The Grand Theatre, Byker. A lovely old Edwardian theatre. You'll get on well there.'

I thought, well, it's better than nothing, I suppose. Who runs the company? I asked. 'Charlie Denville.' I didn't know who Charlie Denville was. What does he do there? Dodie Smith? St. John Irvine? Miriam shook her head. 'Oh, no, dear. Melodrama. 'The Coastguard's Daughter', 'The Prince and the Beggarmaid', 'Sweeney Todd', The 'Sheikh of Araby', and so forth!'

Oh, that's different, isn't it? Yes,' she agreed, 'that's quite different.' Right. When do I start?

'Next week.' That's fine, I said. How much?

'Five pounds, dear. All my artists get five pounds a week until they are worth more.'"

Kenny enjoyed the excitement and the challenge of Byker but after seven months, with two performances a night and two different plays a week, he felt he would be stuck there if he did not move on. Back to Miriam Warner he went.

"*I told her that I did not want to play blood-and-thunder melodrama all my life. I wanted to have a go at Shaw and Shakespeare, at the parts actors must play before they can genuinely claim to be actors. Miriam heard me out patiently.*

'I'll think about it,' she said. 'At the moment, there is a revival of James Parrish's play 'Distinguished Gathering' at King's Theatre, Hammersmith. There is the part of an airman which might suit you.'

This was based on the character of Jim Mollison, the husband of the famous woman pilot, Amy Johnson.

I read for the part, and I got it. We had a two-week run in Hammersmith, and all the time kept telling ourselves that even if Hammersmith might not be quite the West End, it was very nearly West End. A lot nearer than Byker, in any event.

During these two weeks, Miriam persuaded Derek Salberg, the general manager of the Grand Theatre in Wolverhampton, to come and see me in the play. Derek's father was Leon Salberg, a theatrical impresario in the Midlands, who owned the Royal Alexandra Theatre, Birmingham, and had a long lease on the Grand Theatre, Wolverhampton.

Derek Salberg was looking for a juvenile lead for the Grand, and he came backstage and offered me a job for the next season, which would start in a month's time. I was terribly excited, and went to see Miriam to ask her how much money he would pay me.

'A fiver, dear, she replied shortly.'

This was less than I had made nearly a year earlier at the Windmill.

When am I going to get some more money, for God's sake? I asked her.

'When you deserve it, you will get it,' she said dryly. 'In the meantime, you should thank God you are getting that much. Don't criticise me. Just be thankful you are receiving a fiver a week. Lots of actors aren't and would like to.'

The Grand, Wolverhampton, was everything The Grand, Byker, was not. It was efficient and smoothly run – by Salberg's cousin, Basil Thomas – and we all had proper scripts. We had two performances every evening, as at Byker, but each play ran for a whole week. Every morning and afternoon, we rehearsed the following week's play, and in our spare time we learned our lines for the play for the week after next. It was a happy company...

The end of this tour coincided with the end of the pantomime season, and I returned to Wolverhampton. I was not too keen about staying in repertory for another season, but I had no other offer. This time I did break the five pounds limit and my salary went up to seven pounds ten shillings a week – quite a considerable sum in those days. But even so, I was conscious that time was passing, and, as at Byker, I felt I had to make a break for bigger things or I might be trapped in repertory for ever. Yet I do not know how long I might have stayed at Wolverhampton if war had not intervened and solved the problem for me. When it came, in September 1939, I immediately went to the recruiting office in Birmingham to volunteer for the Navy..."

4

"If all the world's a stage I have, in real life, played
many parts: engineering apprentice, shop assistant,
emigrant to Canada, stagehand, naval officer,
clubman.And in the make-believe world of stage and
films and TV I have played many more: medical
student, legless pilot, businessman, barrister, man
of property, inn keeper and priest..."
Kenneth More

With the outbreak of war, and following a stint with the Merchant Navy onboard HMS *Lobus* ('a sea going Genevieve', as Kenny would call it), he soon found himself aboard the cruiser HMS *Aurora* as its Watch Keeping Officer, before moving on to the gun control platform, operating the ship's 4-inch anti-aircraft guns. His time at sea would end up having the greatest impact on his character and his acting style.

"I reported to Aurora *as soon as I left his office. She was lying alongside one of the docks, and I stood for a moment looking at this sleek cruiser, smart in her dazzle paint. I saw her two funnels, her six six-inch and eight four-inch guns, and all the other short-range and anti-aircraft weapons, and I could hardly believe my good luck. This ship was going to be my home for I knew not how long. I had no idea when or where she would sail, but from now on I was to be part of her company, and her destiny would be mine. It was May 1942.*

When I think back to my years in the Navy, it is as though the incidents I recall must have happened to someone else.

Did I really sail down the Mersey in HMS Aurora on a July morning in 1942, as a Watch Keeping Officer, and then up past Northern Ireland where we were escort ship for a fleet of mine-layers?

Did I peer out with aching, red-rimmed eyes through thick fog at icebergs that loomed like floating cliffs in a world of silence and the sea?

I must have done, and yet it all seems so remote now that it could have taken place in another life; and, in a sense, it did.

After the Battle of Alamein, when Rommel began to retreat in North Africa, we returned to Gibraltar, and hoisted the flag of Sir Andrew Cunningham. We took him to Algiers, and then sailed with him and General Eisenhower for the bombardment of Pantelleria, the Axis naval base in the Sicilian Channel.

We opened fire at half past ten one morning and soon the island was completely covered by smoke. A hundred Flying Fortresses attacked it. The blast from all the explosions was so great that, although we were riding three miles out to sea, Aurora *trembled with the force of the bombardment.*

Back to Algiers, then on to Tripoli to pick up King George VI, to carry him to Malta. After he had been piped aboard, the King talked to each of us about our service careers, and then retired to his quarters in the admiral's cabin. It was intended that he would eat there, but none of us thought he could eat very much, because he was suffering from a complaint that had affected every one of us at one time or another − gyppy tummy. His personal doctor was soon visiting him with a bottle of the familiar white stomach mixture the rest of us already knew so very well. What intrigued me in a theatrical sense was that amid all the royal luggage taken aboard was one black tin trunk, about five feet long, one foot wide and four feet deep. This lay on the deck in the waist of our ship for everyone to see. There was no royal crest on it, no cipher, no name. Instead, on the top in white capital letters were simply stencilled two words: THE KING.

When we returned to Tripoli, we discovered that this trunk contained insignia and mementoes which the sovereign always carried when travelling. As he was about to leave Aurora, *for example, he created our skipper a Commander of the Victorian Order in recognition of the responsibilities he had undertaken in transporting the King, so soon after the siege had been lifted."*

The Captain of the *Aurora*, Bill Agnew, took the decision to have Kenny become the ship's Action Commentator, a unique role to *Aurora*, communicating the goings-on to the crew below during a conflict. Kenny found his acting experience helped him to convey a sense of calm and steady nerves when reporting action to the decks below.

During his personal time onboard Kenny got on well with his shipmates, helping them write wonderfully romantic love letters home to their partners. HMS *Aurora* would journey across the Atlantic and Mediterranean seeing its fair share of battle. Wartime missions aboard HMS *Aurora*, and later, Royal Navy aircraft carrier HMS *Victorious*, would lead Kenny to receive campaign star medals for conflicts in Africa, Italy, the Atlantic and the Pacific.

Whilst at sea on board HMS *Aurora*, a recurring dream Kenny had as a child became a reality:

"From the age of six or seven I had a regularly recurring dream which never altered. In my dream, I was always wearing a naval uniform, and I was lying on the deck of a ship. As I lay, I could hear the sound of engines in the sky, droning like an approaching swarm of bees. The noise made me look up, and I could see an aeroplane right above me. As I watched, a bomb was released from this plane, and began to drop slowly and remorsefully towards me. As it came closer, the bomb grew bigger and bigger until it filled the whole sky. Then, at the moment when it should explode I would awake, sweating, and with a racing heart.

On board the Aurora, *and while I was acting as commentator, the exact circumstances of my dream were reproduced. The look-out reported aircraft were approaching on the port quarter.*

'How many?' asked the captain.

The look-out began to count.

'Two, four, five, six.'

As the figure grew our hearts began to sink.

'Seven, eight, ten, twelve.'

'What are they?' I asked him.

'Stukas, sir. Eighty-sevens. Yellownose.'

Hell, I thought. This meant that the pilots were experienced Channel fliers from Battle of Britain days. We should have little chance.

The look-out counted on remorselessly: 'Fourteen, fifteen. I would say, eighteen, sir, making towards us now. Turning.'

We opened up against them with our main armament of six-inch guns – and hit nothing. We had been in the Mediterranean for two years, and I suppose we were a tired ship. Although we filled the sky with hardware the planes still came on totally undamaged. Speaking into the microphone, so that anyone below decks would know what was happening, I kept nothing back, because I knew instinctively that this was a moment of life or death for many if not all of us.

'Diving now,' I said. 'Fourth plane diving. Third plane's bombs have gone to starboard. Wait...!'

Suddenly, my voice left me, for, looking up in the sky, I saw the exact shape of the plane in my dream. There it hung, directly above me, and as I looked I saw the bomb leave the aircraft as I knew it would, and grow larger and larger. And I knew that this one would hit. I lay down on the deck. There was nowhere to go, nowhere to run to and nothing I could do. In front of me was a Paramount News cameraman, who was filming the action. He did not realise his danger.

'Get down, for Christ's sake!' I yelled, and he threw himself down beside me with all his equipment.

'Move up a bit,' I told him, for we were in the narrow side of the bridge and I barely had room to breathe. He moved, and in that second of moving the bomb hit the ship. It landed absolutely square on the four-inch gun deck aft – exactly where I would have been standing had I not been moved to the bridge to do my commentary. By a miracle we were not killed. A piece of bomb came through the steel protection plates on the lower bridge and gashed the photographer's head. If I hadn't told him to move up he wouldn't have been hit. He took a pretty dim view of this, but he recovered. We both did. I never had that dream again.

Years later, at various times in my career when nothing seemed to be going well for me, on a professional or personal level, I would think back to this incident and it would give me hope. Surely I had not been saved simply to go down elsewhere before my time? And the belief that I had been spared, largely because I had been an actor, would give me new hope and confidence to continue my struggle in this profession."

It was this incident on board *Aurora* which would haunt him for many years to come, reliving the whole affair through many nightmares. Following the battle itself Kenny was put on night watch, trawling through the wreckage to remove body parts of comrades who had been caught up in the attack. It is hard to imagine now what he must have gone through. If he had still been working on gun control as opposed to ship's commentator, he would not have survived, like so many of his fellow shipmates including his successor. Angela More once told me how much of his later struggles he would take in his stride because of his wartime experiences. When you had seen the sorts of things Kenny had during wartime, like so many others of his generation, you understand why.

"*While everyone else was celebrating the end of the war in London, I was in a troopship,* Nieuw Amsterdam, *in the Red Sea, on my way to the Pacific to join the aircraft carrier* Victorious.

We worked with the American fleet, and converged for what we believed would be the final air bombardment of Japan. We would refuel at sea, miles from anywhere. In fact, we sailed for fifty days without seeing any land whatever, our aircraft constantly bombing the mainland. Then came the news that the atom bombs had been dropped. For four days we waited, until word of the Japanese acceptance of Allied peace terms came through.

The relief that swept through Victorious *was tremendous. No more war. We had a hundred Fleet Air Arm pilots on board, and we all drank ourselves silly in a phenomenal party. It was summer, and hot, and we took off our clothes. Finally, from the commander down, we were all stripped stark naked. There were men hanging from the bulkheads, and up among the pipes, all singing uproariously. Such a party had its dangers. When we finished a drink, we merely dropped the bottle or glass on the deck. Next morning we all reported sick with cut feet. And next morning, too, we realised the war was officially over. Our gunnery officer was a regular naval officer and a real stickler. The day after the war ended, he put up a notice: 'All brass on guns will now be polished.' And, with various degrees of enthusiasm, or lack of it, we polished our way back to Britain.*

Although we were delighted that the war was over, those of us who, like me, had not become established in our careers before it had started so long ago, now felt some murmurs of unease. What would things be like when we got home? Would we be able to pick up the threads of careers we had abandoned so lightheartedly in 1939? Could we still make it?"

5

"Of course, I believe totally in the character when I am acting. I become that person. But when the moment passes of wearing someone else's skin, and saying someone else's words, I can switch off immediately."
Kenneth More

January 1946 saw Kenny released from the Royal Navy. He was handed a gratuity of £146 from a Post Office savings account to aid his return into society. First stop was a clothing establishment in Earl's Court, who were helping to equip ex-servicemen. Kenny was limited with what he could pick up and came away with a sports jacket, flannels, shoes, a raincoat, a blue and white tie and a green pork pie hat. It must have felt overwhelming to return to London after so much time at sea with little or no acting contacts, in a country which must have seemed very different to the one he left to serve.

It was a man called Geoffrey Robinson who was instrumental in helping Kenny find and sign with agent Harry Dubens. Geoffrey had taken it upon himself to act as a go-between for actors returning from the war and agents looking for new clients. Harry was strictly seeking those who had served at the front, most likely because of their wartime experiences and due to the fact that they had been out of work for so long. Kenny and Harry both got on well and a deal was struck over a handshake. A long and fruitful working relationship was to follow:

"Here was a man who had always expressed his faith in me, right from my very first meeting when I went to see him in 1946, still wearing my naval uniform. He had guided me well and loyally through all kinds of disappointment and achievements. And whenever I sought advice, no matter at what hour of the day or night, he would always give his wise counsel."

Kenny would return to the theatre, appearing in 'The Crimson Harvest' (1946) at the Gateway Theatre, Notting Hill. It was here that BBC producer Michael Barry saw Kenny and offered him a contract to star in small television plays at the Alexandra Palace to help restart the BBC.

Jenny Laird and John Fernald's 'And No Birds Can Sing' (1946) marked Kenny's West End debut at the Aldwych Theatre, playing the part of the Reverend Arthur Platt. Within a year he was back on stage in 'Power Without Glory' (1947) by Michael Hutton at the New Lindsey, Notting Hill Gate. It was so well received that it led to a live version being broadcast on the BBC. That same year the legendary English playwright, Sir Noël Coward cast Kenny as a British Resistance Leader, in 'Peace in Our Time', a story of what might have happened if Britain had lost the Second World War. The play opened at the Lyric Theatre. Kenny and Noël Coward got on well and stayed friends throughout their lives. 1950 saw Kenny in 'The Way Things Go' by Frederick Lonsdale at the Phoenix Theatre, alongside a cast which included Michael Gough, Glynis Johns, Ronald Squire and Janet Burnell.

His first breakthrough came on stage at The Duchess Theatre in 1952, playing the role of Freddie Page alongside Peggy Ashcroft in Sir Terence Rattigan's 'The Deep Blue Sea'. The production had previously run in Brighton and Cardiff before transferring to the West End. It was noted actor and friend Ronald Culver who had put Kenny forward for the part having known Rattigan. 'The Deep Blue Sea' was a huge success and Kenny received great critical acclaim for his performance. He would often cite it as his favourite stage performance.

"Critics hailed me (in 'The Deep Blue Sea') almost as an overnight discovery, conveniently forgetting I was already thirty-eight, and that

I had been working in the theatre for nearly twenty years...I was late to arrive, and while I knew that at last I had reached a certain height in my profession, I still felt like a man on an unstable ladder. I could easily fall. What I needed urgently was to consolidate my good fortune before the ladder slipped. I could only achieve this through an audience wider than the theatre. I had to succeed in films."

It was whilst he was performing in 'The Deep Blue Sea' that filmmaker Henry Cornelius came backstage with an offer of a part which would change his career forever. The role was that of Ambrose Claverhouse in a film called 'Genevieve' (1953), starring alongside John Gregson, Dinah Sheridan and Kay Kendall.

Cornelius had remembered Kenny from a screen test he had filmed him in for the part of Lt. E.G.R. (Teddy) Evans in 'Scott of the Antarctic' (1948), which was subsequently directed by Charles Frend. This had been Kenny's first attempt to break into cinema, which had not come to fruition, although plenty of film work followed. Cornelius had also previously cast Kenny in a small role in 'The Galloping Major' (1951).

Kenny had trepidation: *"It can't be done...I can't work all day in the studios and all night on stage. I'll be dead."* Cornelius responded by saying he could not afford to say no to this. Something in the way he conveyed this to Kenny impressed him.

"But why me? You admit you haven't seen me in the play. You don't know anything about my work."

"But I do," Cornelius remarked. *"Do you remember you played a very small part some time ago in a film of mine, 'The Galloping Major', with Basil Radford?"*

Kenny was surprised, as the part had been minuscule. Regardless, Cornelius had remembered him and now he was offering the chance of a lifetime. Kenny signed the contract for a fee of £3,500.

Filming during the day and performing at night on stage took its toll on Kenny, as he recalls:

"I aimed to finish at Pinewood by half past five to give me time to drive to London and change. Then I was due to walk on stage, carrying a set of golf clubs, and say to the woman with whom I was having an affair: 'Hello, Hes. I'm just back from Sunningdale. We did 93 m.p.h. in Johnnie's car.'

On this particular evening, the film director had begged for one more shot before I left for the theatre. I did not want to disappoint him, but the extra shot meant that I was late leaving the studios. The driver of the car planned to make up lost time, but half a mile up the road, we ran into thick fog.

The road ahead was nothing but a mass of stationary red taillights. I could not bear to look at my watch as the minutes ticked away remorselessly, for the time for me to be at the theatre was already past.

The chauffeur doubled downside streets, through housing estates, across roundabouts, and finally, we reached the stage-door. The doorman was outside, looking for me frantically. I raced past him, grabbed my set of golf clubs and went straight on to the stage, without any make-up, without even brushing my hair.

'Hello, Hes. I'm just back from Sunningdale,' et cetera, et cetera."

During this time, Charlie Chaplin came over to London, and saw the play. A party was held in his honour:

"After dinner, Chaplin began to tell stories of his early days in Hollywood, but my eye kept continually going to my wristwatch. Finally, at midnight, like Cinderella, I had to leave.

'I must be up at six-thirty tomorrow for filming,' I explained.

Chaplin was amazed.

'You mean you're playing that part every night on stage and filming in the day as well?'

'That's right,' I admitted. 'Every day.'

'Put your hand on your heart,' Chaplin commanded sternly.

I did so. Then he placed his hand over mine and said gravely, 'Promise me solemnly you will never, never do this again. It will take years off your life. This is death to an artiste.'

I was then beginning to realise what he meant...I was physically and mentally exhausted, and was glad when 'The Deep Blue Sea' ended its run and filming was over..."

'Genevieve' is deemed a British comedy classic today but when production was complete on the film, there was no sign at first of this ever being so. The chief executives at Pinewood decided it was terrible and it had also cost far more than had been expected. Despite this, 'Genevieve' was released into cinemas and ended up being a surprise, runaway success. The public lapped up the London to Brighton car rallying adventure. More's perfect comic timing won the audience over, immediately making him a rising star overnight. 'Genevieve' was the second most popular movie in England that year. It won Best British Film at the 1954 British Academy Awards, as well as a nomination for Kenny for Best British Actor. The film was Oscar nominated in 1955 for Best Story and

Screenplay and Best Music Score. Not a bad result for a movie which was almost never released in cinemas.

'Genevieve' was the film that had captured my imagination as a little boy and it still manages to entertain me exactly the way it did when I first saw it. We see a whole range of characterisation in Kenny's performance. The over-grown adolescent, the hopeless romantic full of boundless charm, and the man who will stop at nothing to win the day. It is simply a treasure. Larry Adler's theme for the film soundtrack to 'Genevieve' is probably one of the catchiest tunes ever to be committed to celluloid.

It was another, soon-to-become comedy classic 'Doctor in the House' (1954), based on the novels by Richard Gordon, which gave Kenny his next great success.

"One morning, I opened a parcel which had come through the post, and found that it contained the script for 'Doctor in the House'. I read this, and knew immediately that it was for me...The success of the film is one of the legends of Wardour Street. It broke all attendance records in London and then throughout Britain, and when it was first shown in America the audience stood up and clapped."

His performance as Richard Grimsdyke, the happy-go-lucky student doctor saw him scoop Best Actor at the 1955 British Academy Film Awards. So many of Ambrose Claverhouse's qualities are alive and well here in Richard Grimsdyke, so much so that one might even consider them relatives. Kenny's BAFTA win was extremely significant in that the award had gone to a comedy performance, something considered a rarity, and one Kenny was especially proud of receiving. His old friend Ronald 'Ronnie' Squire had once told him that you don't win awards for comedy. How things were changing. Kenny's face was now showing up on the covers of some of the best-selling magazines of the day. 'Doctor in the House' was the most popular film at the box office in 1954 and led to a whole raft of sequels.

Following 'Doctor in the House' Kenny was approached by the great director David Lean to star as a young R.A.F. officer in India during wartime, who has a love affair in Delhi with a beautiful Japanese girl. The film, 'The Wind Cannot Read', would be based on the best-selling novel by Richard Mason. It would have been an amazing opportunity but Kenny felt that the audience would not accept him in such a serious role after appearing in 'Genevieve' and 'Doctor in the House'. He turned David Lean down. Both Sir Laurence Olivier and producer Sir Alexander Korda thought he was mad to reject working with Lean. Kenny was adamant he had made the right choice. It was not until many years later that he greatly regretted passing up his chance of working with one of Britain's greatest directors. Kenny often said that Lean had never forgiven him either.

"I wrote a long letter to David Lean in India, and told him why I felt I could not take the part. He did not reply, and I now realise I was virtually implying that I had no faith in his ability to make me believable in a new kind of role. Worse, he scrapped the film. He sold the rights elsewhere, and a shortened and greatly altered version appeared with Dirk Bogarde. This was the greatest mistake I ever made professionally."

In 1955, Kenny appeared in the family comedy 'Raising a Riot', directed by Wendy Toye, who was also a friend. 'Raising a Riot' also reunited him with his father figure, actor Ronnie Squire. Kenny recalls how they encountered the British artist L.S. Lowry whilst filming:

"We were on location on the Thames Estuary in Kent. Wendy Toye has strong links with the north of England, and Lowry the famous painter was a close friend. He came down to spend a few days and made sketches of us all. He pictured me lying down, as usual, for a nap after lunch, and all the men and women in the unit around doing their particular tasks. So we joined the legion of his matchstalk men and matchstalk cats and dogs."

That same year, Kenny returned to the role of Freddie Page in a big-screen version of Terence Rattigan's 'The Deep Blue Sea', this time playing alongside Vivien Leigh. The screen adaptation was produced by Alexander Korda and directed by Anatole Litvak. Incidentally, he had brought the role back to life the previous year for BBC television's Sunday-Night Theatre series.

More's performance in the cinematic screen adaptation was once again praised by audiences and critics alike, leading to being awarded the prestigious Volpi cup for Best Actor at the Venice Film Festival, as well as a nomination for Best Actor at the British Film Academy Awards. Further honours were bestowed by the Variety Club of Great Britain as Most Promising International Star of 1955. He had finally made his mark. Despite all of this, the film was a disappointing experience for Kenny, most notably because he felt there had been a lot of miscasting, in particular with Vivien Leigh. He also felt the film had deviated from Rattigan's work too much. The energy and tension that was so evident on stage had been lost in its adaptation on screen.

It was a serious leading role initially turned down by Richard Burton which would make Kenny the major star he had always hoped of becoming, playing the real-life, legless fighter pilot, Sir Douglas Bader. A living legend.

Kenny had read 'Reach for the Sky', Paul Brickhill's biography of Bader, whilst on holiday in the South of France.

"I was immediately impressed by its possibilities for a film. Bader was a man who never gave up, who adamantly refused to be beaten. He was an athlete of renown, due to play rugby for England, and then he broke his legs in a stupid foolhardy dare, flying a plane too low. Both legs had to be amputated, one above and one below the knee.

He learned to walk with tin legs and refused to use a stick. He taught himself to dance on tin legs; he even flew again − and became one of the great pilots of the Second World War. He was shot down and captured, damaging both his artificial legs. When the Germans sportingly allowed a spare set of tin legs to be dropped by parachute, Bader immediately and impudently used them to try to escape.

Here was a story of humour, pathos and that most rare and rewarding of all human virtues, personal courage. The book moved me so deeply I was convinced I was the only actor who could play this part properly. This sounds very boastful now, but I believed it. Most parts that can be played by one actor can equally well be played by another, but not this. Bader's philosophy was my philosophy. His whole attitude to life was mine. I wanted this part, not just because I felt I could do full justice to it, but because it was an embodiment of my own belief that courage, faith and determination can overcome all obstacles."

Kenny met Bader at Gleneagles, where they played a round of golf together, Bader winning each time. They got on well, which was somewhat surprising given that Bader was not that keen on the film industry. *"Good luck, Ken. I know you can do a good job,"* remarked Bader. Not wanting to caricature him, Kenny kept his distance when preparing for the role, something which impressed Bader.

He worked hard in preparation for the role, starting with lessons with the West London Flying Club. He practised Bader's walk, at first by simply locking in his knees, but he soon realised he needed much more help than this. Kenny went on to the limb rehabilitation centre in Roehampton, who provided him with steel plates and straps to lock the joints in his feet and hold his knees rigid. Kenny was no method actor but he wanted to do everything he could to do justice to Bader. Kenny even took private flying lessons, but the studio wouldn't let him fly solo.

A humorous moment occurred during filming, which Kenny remembered for years to come:

"There is a famous scene when Bader lies in hospital after the flying accident in which he lost both his legs. He is dying. In a kind of coma he dimly hears two young nurses laughing in the corridor outside his room, and then a senior nurse reprimanding them.

'Less noise, please, a young boy's dying in there.

At that moment – in real life, as in the film – Bader realised that everyone had already given him up and written him off. He was as good as dead. This realisation spurred him to recover.

'I'm not going to die – just to please a few nurses in the corridor.'

This was the turning point in his life. We were filming this scene in Pinewood Studios at about half past ten in the morning. At that hour, what we called the tea boat would always come round with cups of tea and coffee and – a great luxury – about eight pieces of bread and dripping. You had to rush to be one of the lucky ones for this, because there were no seconds. I liked my bread and dripping, and had asked my stand-in, Jack Mandeville, to queue up for it.

'Don't you worry, Ken,' he assured me. 'I'll get it for you.'

Thus reassured, I lay back in my hospital bed while we played the scene, with the camera close-up on me and a girl's voice off-screen saying, '... a young boy's dying in there...'

I had to show my thoughts on my face through the merest flicker of an eyelid, a faint, stubborn tightening of my lips. This was the moment of truth, the scene on which the whole film pivoted, and I put everything I had into it.

At the end, when Lewis Gilbert said in a very quiet voice, 'Cut,' I opened my eyes, and I saw that people in the unit were crying, they had been so moved. I had done it in one take. There would be no need for any more. So immediately I leaped out of bed.

Jack! I shouted. Have you got my piece of bread and bloody dripping?

Everybody was in hysterics. They couldn't understand this almost instant transition from acting to reality. But I can switch off easily. Of course, I believe totally in the character when I am acting. I become that person. But when the moment passes of wearing someone else's skin, and saying someone else's words, I can switch off immediately."

'Reach for the Sky' became a smash hit upon release, and the most successful film in the United Kingdom since 'Gone with the Wind' (1939). 'Reach for the Sky' also went on to become the most popular British film of 1956, winning a BAFTA in 1957 for Best Film. Sadly he lost out to Peter Finch in 'A Town Like Alice' for the for Best Actor award.

Playing Bader was the leading role of a lifetime and did however garner him a Best Actor award for from major cinema publication, *Picturegoer* magazine. Laurence

Olivier even wrote to Kenny to say he had been proven wrong in advising him not to take the part.

'Reach for the Sky' did something greater for his career: it showed audiences Kenny was not just suited to comic roles, that he had range as a leading man in dramatic performances. This was his finest hour on screen. The story of Bader also resonated deeply with its audience, as Kenny explains:

"The picture gave all of us associated with it an unexpected bonus: the encouragement it offered people who had lost one leg or both legs through injury or accident. I received hundreds of letters from these people and from their relations, explaining how at first the loss had seemed insuperable. But Bader's example was of immense help in regaining their faith and confidence...Bader gave them courage to fight on, and never to accept defeat by disability."

In later years Kenny would end up calling several of his films 'favourites' in the press, but it is the belief that 'Reach for the Sky' remained his preferred choice and greatest accomplishment on screen. Bader and Kenny would remain close friends right until their final years.

The timeless, uplifting theme music by John Addison manages to capture the spirit of the film and Bader's story perfectly and is still considered by many to be one of the best themes ever written for a British feature film.

Hugely popular films 'The Admirable Crichton' (1957), 'A Night to Remember' (1958), 'The Sheriff of Fractured Jaw' (1958) with Jayne Mansfield, 'North West Frontier' (1959) with Lauren Bacall, and 'The Thirty-Nine Steps' (1959) galvanised his status as one of Britain's most sought-after actors of the decade. Once he was a £5-a-week actor in rep, now he was commanding

£50,000 a film. The eminent British critic Dilys Powell became a great admirer of Kenny's work, making the request: 'A little more, please.' Kenny now had script approval over his films and the ability to choose his own co-stars.

At the height of his fame he was offered several opportunities to go to Hollywood. Two film offers would have seen him acting with Marilyn Monroe. However, with the success he was enjoying at home he did not see the point, or even what he had to offer Tinseltown at this juncture. Kenny made the decision not to pursue what so many other British actors at this time were being drawn to. To many, this was deemed a mistake.

Whilst completing work on 'Reach for the Sky', Alexander Korda offered him his next role in a film adaptation of 'The Admirable Crichton', a project Korda owned the film rights to. Kenny initially was not convinced. He felt the play was very old-fashioned and wouldn't sit well with a modern audience. It was director Lewis Gilbert who managed to convince him by suggesting the focus of the story should all be about the life on a desert island and how Crichton would be seen as a likeable, forward-thinking man who could save the day. By the time Kenny was sold on the idea and had telephoned Korda to say he would accept the part if Lewis would direct, he found out that the great producer had passed away overnight. Kenny was distraught, having considered Korda a friend as well as an important figure in his career. He now knew he had to make the film. To prepare for the role, Kenny even took lessons from his part-time butler, who educated him in the art of warming a masters newspaper so that it felt just right when passing it to him for his morning glance at the headlines. Filming commenced at Shepperton before moving onto the exotic island of Bermuda.

In 'The Admirable Crichton' (alternatively titled 'Paradise Lagoon' in the United States), Kenny underplays the role of the butler to the hilt, who, shipwrecked with the family he is serving, finds it is he who is needed to lead the group. Their roles, or rather classes, become completely reversed. Whilst on location, Kenny would often be filmed in his butler's uniform only from his waist up so that he could wear shorts below to keep him cool in the heat. He almost drowned on location in Bermuda whilst filming off a jetty:

"*The yacht owned by my master in the film, Lord Loam, was supposed to be sinking in a hurricane and as his loyal and imperturbable butler I had to swim ashore in full tails.*

The sea was churned up by outboard motor propellers, and fans created a wind, with the result that the waves pounded the yacht as though a Force 10 gale was raging.

Diane Cilento was the maid, who leaped into the water wearing a period nightdress and nightcap. Being an Australian, Diane's ability to swim could put a fish to shame. I jumped in with her and almost instantly the ridiculous tails of my jacket became waterlogged, and the weight dragged me down beneath the surface. Here I was, trying to play the scene as though I was drowning, and I was bloody well drowning!

I called pitifully to the director, Lewis Gilbert, 'Help! Help!' But he, as a true professional, refused to let reality affect illusion.

'Marvellous!' he cried. 'He's drowning! Kenny's drowning! Keep those cameras turning! What a wonderful shot!'

No one came to my aid as I went up and down in the water, gasping desperately for breath. If it hadn't been for Diane, who kept me afloat, I would not be alive to tell about it. Afterwards, Lewis said, 'I didn't realise you were in real trouble.'"

'The Admirable Crichton' (1957) went on to become the third most popular film at the British box office that year. Despite its out of date class structure, the film holds up incredibly well. The casting is perfect, especially that of Diane Cilento, Sally Ann Howes and Cecil Parker. Kenny would stay friends with Sally Ann throughout his life.

In the big-budget British film 'A Night to Remember' (1958), it is the RMS *Titanic* which is the lead. Kenny plays the heroic role of Second Officer Lightoller, who manages to keep his nerve throughout the disaster, only allowing himself the luxury of shedding tears when rescued by the *Carpathia*. Kenny handles the scene onboard in the makeshift chapel beautifully. Although he has often been cited by many as an actor who often played roles which imbued the British stiff upper lip, Kenny never agreed with this critique of his acting. This scene from 'A Night to Remember' is just one example of how he allowed the emotion of a character to overwhelm him only after the drama had subsided. He would call on this technique again in 'Sink the Bismarck!'

The live action filming of the demise of the Titanic took place at Ruislip Lido, and saw the cast literally thrown into icy depths, as Kenny would recall in vivid detail:

"'Right!' cried Bill (MacQuitty, the producer) 'Everybody ready? In you jump.' Not a man or woman moved. We stood, fully clothed, and still feeling the cold. What it would be like in the lido was

beyond imagination. The water lapped at our feet. The nearest lifeboat bobbed thirty yards away under the lights.

'Come on!' shouted Bill anxiously. 'We haven't got all night.'...

If someone didn't give a lead, no one would jump and the whole night would be a total waste. Worse, we would only have to come back on the following night. I swallowed. It had to be me. 'Come on!' I shouted with a bravado I did not feel. 'Last one in's a cissy!' I leaped. Never have I experienced such cold in all my life. It was like jumping into a deep freeze. The shock forced the breath out of my body. My heart seemed to stop beating. I felt crushed, unable to think. I had rigor mortis without the mortis. And then I surfaced, spat out the dirty water and, gasping for breath, found my voice. 'Stop!' I shouted. 'Don't listen to me! It's bloody awful! Stay where you are!'

But it was too late. The rest were in, swimming, around me, shouting and cursing with the agony of coldness."

'North West Frontier' (1959) saw Kenny filming an epic adventure in India with Lauren Bacall, one of the biggest actresses working in Hollywood. They got on exceptionally well during filming and throughout the entire promotional tour. It is perhaps the only role he played which can be considered that of an action hero, although today the story's context is unsettling due to its historic roots of the British Empire in India. However, at the time the film was a triumph at the box office, leading to three nominations at the 1960 British Film Academy Awards, including Best Film, Best Director and Best Screenplay.

Whilst in Jaipur during the making of 'North West Frontier' (alternatively titled 'Flame Over India' in the United States), an old soothsayer, whose hand had been mightily crossed with rupees, concluded the session with a large wink, and these words to Kenny: "Do not forget… always light your lamp before it becomes dark." This remark stayed with him for the rest of his life.

"The story demanded that rebels should ambush a train in the desert, and we had to set fire to a lot of brush wood near the railway line to keep these rebels at bay. This means that a stunt man impersonating me was due to lie across the rail, already very hot in the sun's heat, and shoot a service revolver at the rebels through flames which were steadily moving closer to him as the bush burned.

The stunt man refused to do this. It was too dangerous, he declared. So I said to the director, Lee Thompson, 'I'll have a go.' And I did.

But that stunt man was no fool. By the time the scene was finished the flames had come so near that they burned off the front of my hair and my eyebrows. From then on, the make up people had to give me pencilled-in hair and new eyebrows.

The film ('North West Frontier') was a great success. I seemed now to be the golden boy or the middle-aged man which could do no wrong. Offers poured in. I was wanted in this play, that film, the other TV series. One paper even carried a headline 'MORE magnificent'. I was riding on the crest of the wave. But soon the wave would break."

A wonderful film adaptation of John Bucan's 'The Thirty-Nine Steps' (1959) concluded the decade of work which saw Kenny cement his reputation as Britain's most popular, and highest paid actor of the 1950s. It was whilst filming 'The Thirty-Nine Steps' that Kenny received word from the director Ralph Thomas that his beloved agent, Harry Dubens, had died. Kenny was heartbroken:

"Here was a man who had always expressed his faith in me, right from my first meeting when I went to see him in 1946, still wearing

my naval uniform. He had guided me well and loyally through all kinds of disappointments and achievements. And whenever I sought advice, no matter at what hour of the day or night, he would always give his wise counsel."

That same year, Kenny was surprised by Eamonn Andrews at the Odeon cinema, Shepherd's Bush, with a television tribute on the popular 'This is Your Life' series. Among the many in attendance were Kay Kendall and the St Bernard from 'Genevieve', Dirk Bogarde from 'Doctor in the House' and Sally Ann Howes from 'The Admirable Crichton'.

The start of the Sixties showed that Kenny was still in great demand as the most popular international star of 1960. In the film, 'Sink the Bismarck!' (1960), directed again by Lewis Gilbert, Kenny plays well beyond type in his characterisation of Captain Shepherd, easily separating it from any other of his dramatic performances. Shepherd leads the Navy task force's search for the Bismarck from the Admiralty's Operations Room. The character remains emotionally cut off for ninety-nine per cent of the film, Kenny drawing heavily on his own experience in the Royal Navy. It is without doubt one of his best accomplishments on screen and a personal favourite of mine. The *Sunday Pictorial* at the time stated: 'Kenneth More gives one of the greatest performances of his career'.

I remember the first time I saw it on VHS. I almost had to question who I was seeing on screen, asking myself 'is that really Kenneth More?' His stoic performance in the film stood very much at odds with the sort of roles I was accustomed to seeing him in.

Despite being incredibly popular both critically and commercially (including in the United States) Kenny's role in 'Sink the Bismarck!' was not commended at any of the major award ceremonies. Filmmakers as well missed a step by not exploiting these characteristics by casting him in roles as unique and captivating as Shepherd. Again, similar to Lightoller in 'A Night to Remember', it is not until the very end of the story that Shepherd allows himself the luxury of shedding tears when finally receiving word that his son is alive.

Incidentally, it was Kenny's real-life ship, HMS *Aurora*, that had become the flagship of the 12th Cruiser Squadron which had earlier played an important part in the search for Bismarck. The squadron had been under the command of Rear Admiral Sir Cecil Harcourt. When filming took place for 'Sink the Bismarck!' Kenny thought it would be a nice gesture to ask Harcourt, as his old admiral, to come to the studio during production. Whilst on the set of the Operations Room, and before Kenny moved a ship on the board, he would ask Harcourt, "*Is that all right, sir? Is that correct.*" Harcourt was delighted. As he left, he shook all the crew by the hand, none more so than Kenny's. "*This has made my day, More*", he said. A few days later, his wife wrote to tell Kenny to tell him that the Admiral had died. More recalled this in his autobiography:

"*He had driven home and as he turned off the ignition in his car, his heart turned off too, and he died at the wheel. I like to think that his last memory of the Navy he served so well was with us.*"

1960 also saw Kenny in the romantic comedy 'Man in the Moon', starring alongside Shirley Ann Field in a film directed by Basil Dearden. It was not well received, and this is probably the first indication that the times were changing, and the style of comedy with it. It is a shame, for although the second half of the film is weak in comparison to the first, Kenny gives another star performance as the happy-go-lucky gentleman who lives life very much on his own terms.

Whilst Kenny was holidaying in the South of France he received a call from director Lewis Gilbert, asking him if he could lose some weight to appear in his new picture, 'The Greengage Summer' (1961), playing Eliot, a loveable romantic with a shady criminal past. The film was going to be shot around Épernay, in the Champagne district of France.

Kenny recounts the telephone conversation:

"'What do you mean? I'm pretty slim.'

'In your body, yes,' Gilbert answered. 'But not your face. You have always had a face like a full moon. Can you lose some weight from your face?'

'What the hell do you mean? I've been a film star with a full moon face for years.'

'But you've never played a romantic part before...You need a slim face for that. Am I making myself clear?' Gilbert retorted.

'You'd better ask Dirk Bogarde or Donald Sinden for romantic stuff. Not me,' Kenny replied.

'I'm not asking them, Ken. I am asking you. We want you to play opposite Susannah York in Greengage Summer... he is supposed to be romantic. So it would be better if she fell in love with someone who hadn't a face like a full moon. Do you follow me?'

'All the way. I'll see what I can do.'"

Kenny went on a diet and upon returning to England, Gilbert decided his face was thin enough. Kenny would later call the making of 'The Greengage Summer' (alternatively titled 'Loss of Innocence' in the United States) as one of the happiest films he had ever worked on, describing Gilbert as *"a very simple person with no side or pretence, and a great technician. He is also extremely efficient, and so extracts efficiency from others. This is not a gift in the possession of all directors."* The film stands the test of time and Kenny looks at his best as the debonair British ex-patriot trying to hide himself away from his past exploits as a criminal. In 1961 he was the third most popular international star.

6

"I could have tried to make a niche for myself by playing character parts of ageing officers or men-about-town or ambassadors, as so many other actors have done in middle life and beyond. But this would only be a treading of already well-trodden ground. Each performance would, of necessity, have been a diminished success, and as success dwindles, so does one's income, and, more important, one's horizons."

Kenneth More

S ome People' for director Clive Donner and 'We Joined the Navy', directed by friend, Wendy Toye, were two films that opened in 1962, neither managing to reclaim Kenny's past glories as a number one box office draw. He was still marked the fourth most popular international star in 1962.

However, when the Swinging Sixties began in 'full swing' they brought about a huge cultural shift within the industry, and the tastes of the public at large. Leading parts which Kenny had always gravitated towards began to diminish on the silver screen and were considered by many to be old fashioned. Moreover, British film, a once thriving industry, was now greatly diminished. Kenny had never wished to go to Hollywood and this decision impacted him. I spoke to Kenny's agent Michael Whitehall exclusively about this: "I think the problem with him was that he really wanted his career to be based here. He wanted to be a film star, which indeed he was, but he didn't want to go to America and be a movie star. He didn't want to follow Rex Harrison and all those people. He wasn't that sort of person and unfortunately that meant that his movie career disappeared. It was almost self-induced. So, then he turned to doing other things. He started doing much more theatre than he had done before."

Kenny was already setting his sights on a return to television. A medium he thought very underrated and could give him much more scope as an actor than the sort of roles he was now being offered on screen. It was 'Heart to Heart' (1962) which saw Kenny play journalist David Mann, who is pitted against cabinet minister Sir Stanley Johnson (played by Sir. Ralph Richardson) in a televised interview. 'Heart to Heart' was written by eminent British playwright Sir Terence Rattigan, who had based this new play on the real-life interview series, 'Face to Face'. The character of David Mann was modelled on the former politician-cum-presenter John Freeman. 'Heart to Heart' was part of 'The Largest Theatre in the World', a project that saw European countries produce their own version of a play, which would be televised across Europe on the same night.

The play holds up incredibly well upon reviewing, especially so with its characterisation of an unsavoury politician who bends the law to his own will. Ralph Richardson is excellent as the politician, and the supporting cast of Jean Marsh, Wendy Craig, Angela Baddeley and Peter Sallis all helped to create a captivating television drama.

In an exclusive interview, Canadian-born director Alvin Rakoff, now 93 and as sharp as an arrow, recalled the making of the show: "It was no small feat for television to have an author of that stature (Rattigan), writing especially for television. Every nation in Europe was supposed to do their own production of it, and most of them did, and then they were to be compared. It was a Eurovision song contest for plays. Richard Burton agreed to play the lead and Rattigan and I met him in Rome. He was doing 'Cleopatra' with Elizabeth Taylor at the time. Up until a couple of weeks before we were going to start rehearsal things dramatically changed when Burton suddenly said no. So we were stuck. Then Rattigan said he would call on his friend, Kenny More, and he stepped in to play the part. Kenny and I got on very well."

Wendy Craig, a wonderful actress who played the character of Production Secretary Jessie Weston, whom Kenny falls in love with, spoke exclusively to me about working with Kenny: "I adored him. I loved his work. I thought he was an absolutely brilliant actor. It was very exciting for me to be working with him. It was overwhelming really. He was a very big star. He was exactly as he appeared on screen. He was urbane, charming, funny, with a very beautiful voice and the most lovely delivery...twinkling brown eyes...he was all I thought he would be. Kenny was a huge presence in the film industry, almost the backbone of it at one time, but he was quite a humble man, quite quiet and modest. I remember he had this lovely convertible sports car, which I admired. He gave me a lift home once, he was just such a lovely person. I felt very comfortable working with him because he was a professional down to his fingertips. We would rehearse the scene a few times and find our positions but we worked so well together that we didn't have to analyse everything, it just came very naturally. It was a joyful experience because when you are working with an actor who is comfortable in his own skin and knows what he is doing, is intelligent and totally at home with the part he is playing, well it's a great pleasure."

In 1963, Darryl Zanuck was making a film in France about the D-Day landings, to be called 'The Longest Day', and he wanted More to play the role of real-life beach-master Commodore Colin Douglas Maud DSO. It was a small cameo, as many were in the film, but it featured a 'who's who' of the leading acting world, and it helped to lift Kenny's spirits at a time when screen roles in major films were few and far between. It's safe to say Kenny had a special affinity for playing real-life heroes.

Maud even lent Kenny the actual shillelagh (wooden club) that he carried ashore in the invasion.

The following year, Kenny gave a masterclass performance in a film adaptation of Douglas Hayes' novel, 'The Comedy Man' (1964). It's his final leading role on film and one of his last attempts at paying the ageing juvenile, something which had clearly run its course in his acting career. However, the part about an actor struggling to find work of quality was something which resonated with him at this point in his life, as Kenny explains:

"I read the script and was profoundly struck by its relevance to my own life, and to the lives of so many actors I had known. It described the experiences of a middle-aged repertory actor who comes to London in a last bid to find the success that has eluded him all his life in the provinces."

It was Kenny who had asked for Alvin Rakoff to direct the film. The two had got on well on 'Heart to Heart'. Alvin Rakoff again: "Kenny understood Chick Byrd completely. Getting past 40 and thinking, as most people do at 40, is it all over? Is it a downward slope from here on in? Little realising the fact that it can be an upward slope... Kenny understood his fellow actors, but he was not a tortured actor. He was not one to rip himself apart in order to do a scene, that wasn't Kenny. He did not intellectualise. We talked briefly about attitude. He knew sadness, he knew happiness and he knew in-between, and so he would call on that. Kenny was so affable that everybody who worked with him adored him.

"We only deviated from the book with the opening of the film. Neither screenwriter Peter Yeldman nor I could work out how to open the picture. It was actor Anthony Booth who had told me a story about a young actor leaving a rep company who had made a final curtain speech to the audience about how he had seduced the producer's wife. I said to Anthony, 'that's it, I am going to use that as the opening for a film I'm working on.' I told the story to Peter and he wrote the scene which appears in the film. Incidentally, we shot that scene at the Richmond Theatre in Surrey."

It would be a long while before 'The Comedy Man' would reach an audience, eventually turning up as a double bill with 'Lord of the Flies'. A strange pairing of films if ever there was one. Elspeth Grant for *Tatler* wrote, 'This is [Kenneth More's] best performance to date, and it is a mystery why the film has been kept in cold storage for eighteen months.'

Kenny had returned to the theatre as early as 1960, directing 'The Angry Deep', a war tale by Anthony Kimmins. It opened at the Theatre Royal in Brighton before touring several regions. It would remain his only directorial experience. 1963 saw him back on stage and starring alongside Celia Johnson in 'Out of the Crocodile' at the Phoenix Theatre. The play reunited him with Johnson, having worked with her previously in 'The Deep Blue Sea', Johnson taking the role of Hester whilst Peggy Ashcroft was away on holiday.

In 1964 Bernard Delfont and Arthur Lewis approached Kenny with the offer of reprising his role as Crichton in a musical version of J.M. Barrie's shipwreck story, co-starring this time with Millicent Martin in 'Our Man Crichton' at the Shaftesbury Theatre. Kenny would have been the first to admit he was no singer, but British impresario Bernard Delfont talked him into it, as Kenny remembers:

"'Have I got to sing much?' I asked him.

'No,' he said. 'You take a few lessons and you'll be all right. So long as you can put a number over.'

'I can put a number over, if I can speak it,' I told him.

'Fine. Speak it to music. I'll get Millicent Martin to play Tweeny. Have a go.'

I had a word with my agent, Laurence Evans, and asked his opinion.

'Before you decide, let's see what we can get for you, Kenny.'

What he got for me was £1,000 a week for the run of the show in lieu of ten per cent of the gross takings; a lot of money.

'But Laurie,' I protested. 'I can't sing.'

'Well,' he said, 'for a thousand a week, anybody can!'

Before the show opened I had three weeks of lessons with a singing teacher. As a result of these, I could cope with the point numbers, which don't require much of a voice, but simply a personality and a manner, but I had a serious ballad I had to sing to Lady Mary, who was played by Patricia Lambert. This was a love ballad and I was so terrible that I asked the producer to take it out of the show. It was essential for the action, however, so it had to remain. I got away with it on most nights, I think, but only just. Pat has a beautiful voice and she covered me so well that I would just come in now and then with a word or a line or a gesture.

On the week of Churchill's funeral, business was very bad. People stayed away from the theatre because their thoughts were about the death of a man who had for so long symbolised so much that was fine in our country. But the show had to go on, although on the Wednesday matinée I saw I was singing this ballad to a house three-quarters empty.

I looked across the orchestra pit to the front row of the stalls and was about to warble, 'And I love you', or words to that effect, when I saw, to my horror, Noël Coward in the circle with Graham Payn on one side and Cole Lesley on the other. Noël's eyes met mine. He shook his head slowly from side to side as though to say, 'Dear boy, that is absolutely terrible. Don't ever do it again.'

I immediately dried up. I could no more finish the song than I could have flown. Pat took up my lines and finished it for me. Afterwards, Noël came round to see me in my dressing-room.

'Dear boy,' he said gravely. 'That was absolutely terrible. Don't ever do it again.'

Despite this, we ran for six months. But I took Noël's advice. I never have done it again."

Around this time, and up until 1967, Kenny struggled. The first protracted period in his career since he had become a star. He still worked but major leading roles had faded for many reasons, both personally and professionally. More than anything, he was now a lot older, time had moved on and he had to seriously rethink the direction he would have to take his career. For some time, he had been looking for a role that could showcase his versatility as an actor. Something to show everyone that he could do more than just playing the happy-go-lucky gentleman, which the public had grown accustomed to despite the varied roles he had already played. It would be the BBC producer Donald Wilson who would throw him the lifeline he needed, offering him a character to play which would end up bringing him the worldwide fame he had never quite achieved in his career up until this point.

"At fifty, a man must come to terms with himself, and look back on what he has done and consider what he can hope to do. He must equate practicalities with dreams. At fifty, I had begun to wonder privately whether my star was indeed on the wane...I had been almost passed by, and I could see no way in which I could fight back. Worse, the will to fight back was itself diminishing. I had taken the popular image of Kenneth More, the extrovert, the perennial beer-drinker and good fellow, as far as it could go. Peter Pan was always young, but I had the mind, and − sometimes more dangerous for an actor − the face of maturity.

I could have tried to make a niche for myself by playing character parts of ageing officers or men-about-town or ambassadors, as so many other actors have done in middle life and beyond. But this would only be a treading of already well-trodden ground. Each performance would, of necessity, have been a diminished success, and as success dwindles, so does one's income, and, more important, one's horizons.

I was not seeking to build a reputation, only to hold what I had already achieve, and, if possible, to consolidate my gains. I needed a role which would be a shop window for my talents. I wanted people to see for themselves what I could do, that I was not limited by a sports jacket and a laugh or by the confines of a uniform in a studio ship. Jolyon (Forsyte) would give me the chance of ageing from early thirties to mid seventies. It is usually easy for a young actor to play an old man, but it is the mark of the professional when an older actor plays someone half his age. This was the challenge I knew I must accept. In a sense, what Donald Wilson was offering me was the longest audition in the world. Well, I had undergone auditions before, and although here the audience would be in tens and finally hundreds of millions, it was still an audience of individuals. The chips were down. This was my chance – perhaps my last chance – to pick them up and play on."

Donald Wilson's adaptation of John Galsworthy's 'The Forsyte Saga' (1967) brought together a magnificent cast who seemed almost born to play the parts they were cast in, none more so than those inhabited by the characters embroiled in the ménage à trois: Kenneth More as Young Jolyon, Eric Porter as Soames and Nyree Dawn Porter as Irene. On paper, the idea of adapting a period story of an upper-middle-class family for television would seem at odds with modern tastes, somewhat not unlike what Kenny first struggled with when offered a part in the big-screen adaptation of 'The Admirable Crichton'. However, this was not what 'The Forsyte Saga' was really about. It was the story and ultimate legacy of a family whose place in society is rattled by their own relationships with one another, often leading to scandal. Family fortune, who had it, and who was chasing it, was often part of the ever unfolding story.

Actor Martin Jarvis would play Kenny's son in the period drama, Jolyon 'Jon' Forsyte. In his book, *From Acting Strangely*, he recalls his memories of Kenny and the production:

"He was an authentic British film star. I was thrilled to be working with one of my idols, the ebullient hero of 'Reach for the Sky', 'Genevieve' and 'The Deep Blue Sea'. Once, on a schoolboy trip to London in the late fifties, I had been walking up the Haymarket with my friend Dave Nordemann, on our way to gaze at the voguish black-and-white Angus McBean production photos outside the Theatre Royal, when we spotted a great beige Rolls Royce coming slowly down the street towards us. The passenger window had been wound down and a tanned figure in a colourful Hawaiian shirt, arm resting casually half in and half out, was grinning and chatting loudly to the chauffeur as they purred along. Kenneth More giving his public a good look at him.

"Although Eric Porter had the number one leading role of Soames Forsyte, it was Kenny who was treated very much as the star of the Saga. (At least until the first episodes were transmitted, after which Eric and Nyree became stars in their own right.) I could see that the production team were enraptured to have this hugely recognisable character in their midst and loved saying, 'Morning Kenny, Cheers Kenny, Martin, do you know Kenny?', and blushed with pleasure when he hailed them blithely, remembering all their names. I soon got the feeling that Kenny himself was much relieved to have secured the part of Young Jolyon Forsyte, though his character departed, after an affecting death scene, in my third episode, number fifteen.

"Kenny's natural screen acting was an education for me. I watched him like a hawk during rehearsals and was intrigued to see how, with apparent truth and simplicity, he related every moment of his character's behaviour to the camera."

'The Forsyte Saga' guaranteed Kenny £15,500 for six or seventh months' work, with a share in any world sales. He would often call the production the happiest he had ever worked on.

"Sometimes, when one does a TV production, the cast is sent along to Morris Angel or Monty Berman, the theatrical costumiers, and they can, if necessary, be issued with clothes off the peg. There was nothing of that sort here. I was measured for four suits before we even started.

When we travelled on location we did not have a caravan to change in; we changed into our costumes in cars, and sometimes even knocked on the front doors of houses nearby and asked if we could use their lavatory, but everyone showed a rare and genuine enthusiasm for the whole project. Because of the cost, most of the exterior work and filming country backgrounds was done in Richmond Park, and had to be compressed into three weeks in June when it was calculated that the weather would be as good as it ever is in Britain. In fifteen working days therefore we had to shoot all the background exteriors for the first fifteen episodes.

Some of the later scripts were not even written, so Donald Wilson had to keep in the back of his mind ideas for backgrounds which could be filmed in advance.

We rehearsed the interiors in a drill hall in Ealing, week after week; two weeks of rehearsals and then three days in the studio to record. We were expected to know all our lines by the tenth day of rehearsal. Lines were chalked on the floor to represent wardrobes, sideboards and beds until props arrived about the sixth day. These were not the final props we would have in the studio, but a big box would represent a chest of drawers and a smaller one a chair and so on, to give the cast a sense of the size of the real furniture.

I would arrive at the drill hall at ten o'clock each morning. Work would begin immediately. We would break at one o'clock for lunch in a café or pub, then would work through the afternoon until 5.30. The drill hall had a room which had been the sergeants' mess and here we could have a drink and manipulate the fruit machine. We did not all rehearse at the same time, and those of us working out a scene would hear our off-duty colleagues playing this machine and listen for the peculiar clank it gave when it paid out the jackpot. Whenever this happened – which it did several times during each week's rehearsals – we would all rush out and congratulate the winner. Usually he or she would buy a round of drinks to celebrate.

Eric Porter, who was playing Soames magnificently, was known for a disinclination to spend two pennies when one penny would do. We all said that if he won the jackpot we'd stop everything for a round of drinks. Sure enough, just before lunch one day we heard the clank of coins pouring out. We stopped work at once and ran into the bar. There he was, counting out his sixpences and shillings into a funny little hat he always wore, like a Dutch engine-driver's cap. We grouped about him waiting for him to buy a round. But this was not to be.

'Thank goodness, I won't have to go to the bank this afternoon,' was all he said, and gave us a beaming smile. The laugh was on us.

After Episode 15 I was free, while the rest still had several more months of work. I had no immediate financial problems, but equally, I had no idea how 'The Forsyte Saga' would go, because it would not be shown for some months."

A scene where Irene plays Debussy's 'Clair de Lune' to Jolyon, ends with Kenny asking for 'More, please'. It would sum up the audience reaction to the series, for when it aired: 'The Forsyte Saga' became a huge, international success, surprising many, including Kenny.

Suddenly, almost overnight, his star was higher than it had ever been in his career.

"It was an extraordinary feeling to be at the centre of all the publicity and excitement about the series. I had discovered with amazement that Nyree Dawn Porter, Eric Porter and Susan Hampshire and I were being talked about in nearly every home in the land. Very soon, we would be talked about in nearly every home in the world.

Two stories show how extraordinarily popular this series was, not only in this country, but everywhere. Its appeal was truly international. Harold Wilson was Prime Minister then, and his government had invited a Yugoslav trade delegation to London. He held a reception for them at No. 10 Downing Street."

Susan Hampshire, who starred as Fleur Mont née Forsyte, spoke to me exclusively about Kenny's attachment to the series and the success of 'The Forsyte Saga': "He was a HUGE star at the time, and the BBC was so lucky to get him. I remember he was a very warm, positive influence at the read-throughs. Not only was Kenny ideal casting (as Young Jolyon) but l am sure his being in the series helped get the drama off to a flying start. When I joined the cast, Margaret Tyzack (who played Aunt Winifred) said she thought the series was very special and going to be an enormous success. How right she was!

"The audience adored Kenny and the viewing figures for the series reached up to 18 million. Church service times were changed so that the viewers could go to mass and be back in time to watch the series (no recording then of course). When Nicholas Pennal (who played Michael

Mont) and l were invited to Sweden to do a publicity tour for the second showing of 'The Forsyte Saga', the crowds greeting us at the airport, and lining the streets, were in their thousands, as though we were the Beatles!"

Around the world 'The Forsyte Saga' became the television event that everyone was talking about. Angela More remembers visiting a church in Madrid at Christmas time with Kenny. "Whispers amongst the parishioners went around fast that he was there. 'It's Jolyon Forsyte!' We couldn't believe it. We made a hasty exit, but it proved he would now be recognised anywhere we went, not just in England. Literally, anywhere!"

"Metaphorically, I could raise two fingers at anyone, and everyone who had belittled me. I knew if I made the grade on TV, I would be seen by more people in one night than would ever gather together to see the greatest films ever made, in the longest run on record...The wheel was still turning. I was on my way back...I had gone through the valley and at last I was out into the sunshine beyond."

7

"Acting can drain a person emotionally and physically, and when you are very tired you are always cold. When an actor comes back late at night from the theatre or a TV or film studio he is cold and weary, and the first thing he thinks about is having a hot bath...Whenever I feel lonely or depressed, I run a hot bath and lie back in it, remembering days when I could not afford such indulgence. This is not only good for the soul – it cures my depression!"
Kenneth More

I *see my own life in two stages. The first stage is of early struggle, when I changed from engineering to a job I really wanted to do. Then came the war, the Navy, and six years doing something entirely different. When I returned to acting I was that much older, and while I had changed, so had the whole world, and especially my chosen profession.*

The second stage in my life began with the extraordinary telephone call from Bob Lennard on a Saturday morning. I had prayed for a clear sign, and a clear sign I was given. So far as I was concerned, this was destiny. Why else should I have been chosen out of hundreds of better-known actors?

That call changed my whole life, because if I had not received it, on the Monday of the following week I should have returned to the Navy. Instead, on that Monday, I was standing on a high shelf in a 'prison' in Hemel Hempstead.

Up to that telephone call, life had been a harsh struggle and a fight for survival. After that call, my rent was paid for two months and my whole career sailed out of the doldrums. Since then I have mercifully never been short of money, although I still have the fear that one day I might be.

All actors and actresses know this fear far more acutely than people in secure jobs. It tends to make them either over-generous or over-mean; or, to be more polite, over cautious in their spending."

It was William Douglas-Home's play, 'The Secretary Bird' (1968), which turned out to be the biggest stage success of Kenny's career. Sir Harold Hobson, writing for the *Sunday Times* said: 'Mr More's performance is not only irresistibly amusing, it is morally beautiful...All his jokes succeed. He is the delight of the entire theatre.' Kenny was so pleased by the reaction to the play: "*From the opening night we played to fantastic business at the Savoy. I also claim that we put the Savoy Grill back on the map as a smart place to eat.*" The following year, 1969, saw his services called upon again for a one-off television version of 'The Secretary Bird' for the series 'Theatre Date'.

1969 also saw Kenny appearing in the war epic, and future screen classic, 'Battle of Britain'. Kenny recalls how he was cast in the small part of a group captain and station commander: "*Having played Bader – whom I met again during the making of this film – they could not contemplate an R.A.F. film of this size without my taking some part! But now, of course, I was too old to play an active pilot.*" 'Battle of Britain' would also see him reunite with actress Susannah York, since 1961's 'The Greengage Summer'.

Further supporting roles on the silver screen followed, including in Richard Attenborough's 'Oh What a Lovely War', 'Fraulein Doktor' (both 1969), and 'Scrooge' (1970), where he was even called upon to sing again in the part of the Ghost of Christmas Present. Kenny was continuing to excel on stage, in a revival of Terence Rattigan's 'The Winslow Boy' (1970), 'Getting On' by Alan Bennett (1971) and 'Sign of the Times' (1973). The theatre, his first home, had once again saved him. It would have seemed a lifetime ago to Kenny since that day in 1935 when he had climbed the stairs of the Windmill theatre looking for work...

Kenny's agent from 1969 until the end of his career was Michael Whitehall, who had taken over the reins from his senior, Laurence Evans. "He was very big. When I said to my mother I was involved with Kenneth More she thought I had made it. To her he was as big a star as you could possibly be. I particularly liked Kenny because he was just a very likeable and charming man. I always remember he was the very first person to tell me to call him by his Christian name. He was a great favourite of mine. I was involved with him when he did all those plays...'Getting On', 'Sign of the Times', 'In Praise of Love' (for television), which he was wonderful in with Claire Bloom...and when he did 'The Slipper in the Rose'.

"I think probably his best work was done in the theatre, and not just his light comedy. He was a very moving, very touching actor...He was very believable on stage, very emotional and could make you cry...He was able to turn on the other side of his talent and become a serious actor. All those Terence Rattigan plays he was particularly strong at. I think that was really where he was at his best, on the stage.

"He was always being asked by the National Theatre to do Shakespeare or classical plays and he would always say to me 'Oh no darling, I don't want to go to the National or the Royal Shakespeare Company.' He had no ambitions in that way at all. He was an absolutely commercial actor. He did not want to join a company. I remember he was asked by several people over the years, Peter Hall and others, and it would always be 'No thank you darling.'"

Whitehall remembers many happy times with Kenny: "There was a lot of socialising in the evening... I was unmarried living on my own in London. We would meet in some restaurant or go to a club together. He had lunch at the Garrick most days... I found it difficult to keep up with him and I was 29. You'd meet him at the Garrick at 12.30 and have a couple of large gin and tonics, then you would go down to lunch and you would have some white wine, and then a bottle of red, and then afterwards back upstairs for a glass of port. I would go back to the office around 15.00 and I could hardly stand up. Kenny would just keep going and then he would probably be off in the evening! He could hold his drink; I never saw him drunk. He had a great capacity for entertaining. He used to stand in the corner of the bar at the Garrick club, which people used to call 'Kenny's corner' because he was always there chatting to his friends. There was talk at one stage, mainly from me, for somebody to put up a brass plaque set into the bar saying, 'In Memoriam, Kenneth More'…but I couldn't get that through."

Kenny was appointed a Commander of the Order of the British Empire in the 1970 New Year Honours. Having been a great royalist, meeting many of the Royal Family over the years, to be awarded a CBE by the highest British institution in the land made him immensely proud.

1974 saw the Kenneth More Theatre open its doors to the public for the very first time with previews of 'The Beggar's Opera'. The theatre officially opened in 1975. For a living actor to have a theatre named in their honour was very rare, and further evidence of him becoming a national icon. Three years later the Kenneth More Theatre staged an evening of poetry, prose and music, with the event 'Kenneth More Requests the Pleasure of Your Company' (1977). He was thrilled to be able to say he had performed on stage at his very own theatre. At their request Kenny even wrote a poem: 'An Ode to a Theatre'. The original version that had been tapped out on Kenny's typewriter was recently unearthed in the archives and handed back to the estate. The poem is published here overleaf for the very first time.

'An Ode to a Theatre' by Kenneth More

Tonight a theatre is born
Not like a Phoenix from some past and fiery lair
But as a muse
Rising from the ground
Built with love and care.

A place to dream
A home for make believe
Where hands that daily reach for supermarket shelves
can change their rhythm
To create...conceive...
Where voices used for daily shouts and crys...
May mellow...alter pitch....
And rise in song.
To reach the skies.

Here…on this stage…all men may play at kings.
Snatching from the humdrum of their lives
Moments of pleasure…temporary power…
Laughter…happiness…so many things.

Dark economic blight and business cares
Must bow to ageless talent
The words of masters…long since dead and others living
Here to grasp...just climb the stairs.

The substance of ambition
Is but the shadow of a dream
Here...dreams come true.
For him…for her…for me...for you.

The poem (one of a few he wrote) is probably the best example in existence of how good a writer Kenny was. He even felt that in another life he could have been a journalist.

Vivyan Ellacott, who ran the Kenneth More Theatre at the time, recalls working with Kenny. "The first time I met him was when he came for the topping out ceremony...he gave a performance, the star, absolutely charming...it was all quite formal. A couple of days later he rang up and asked if we could meet and have a chat. And suddenly what you got in private was a totally different man. In private you got enthusiastic, really excited about the theatre, rather humble and surprised, not quite understanding why it had been named after him. Privately he was never grand. He said to me once, 'can you imagine what it must feel like to walk into a building called the Kenneth More Theatre!' He would never have admitted that in public. One thing that excited him was to travel on the underground to get here! On the way back I would drive him to his house in Notting Hill, and on that long journey he would share stories of people he had met and worked with. But that took time for him to trust me."

In 1974 the TV Times magazine awarded Kenny Best Actor for his performance in the title role of the television series, 'Father Brown'. Based on the books by G. K. Chesterton about a Roman Catholic Priest who solved murder mysteries. Kenny's portrayal won him a whole new audience, some of whom had never seen his earlier cinematic work. Producer impresario Lew Grade was so adamant More was the only choice to play Father Brown for television that he would ring him at home saying:

"Good morning, Father, how are you today Father?" Kenny at first was not convinced that he was right for the part, but finally acquiesced upon speaking to his agent. He was pleased that he did, citing it as one of his best working experiences.

Being associated with the role of Father Brown led to one strange encounter Kenny would recall:

"Some years ago, when I was working in Spain on a film of Verne's 'Journey to the Centre of the Earth', I was stopped by an old peasant woman with a most unusual request. She wanted me to hear her confession. I explained through an interpreter that I was neither Catholic nor a priest, but this did not put her off. She had seen me as 'Padre Brown' in the 'Father Brown' TV series, then showing in Spain with phenomenal success; and as she had bad legs and the place was remote and mountainous, and she hated her parish priest who lived way down the hill, she decided that I was her man. In fact, it was me or no one. Unable to oblige, I left the poor old soul muttering to herself about the inconsistencies of actors. If a man plays the part of a priest, why can't he really be one?"

I had the pleasure of meeting actor Ronald Pickup, who guest starred in the 'Father Brown' episode, 'The Eye of Apollo'. Ronald is a widely acclaimed actor of stage and screen, a warm and kind-hearted man who was very generous with his time. "For me, working with Kenny was just such a joy. He was one of my generation's favourites, and there was something completely seamless from the personality I knew of on-screen from both cinema and television, to the one I worked with. I had met him previously working with Angela Douglas on the TV series, 'The Dragon's Opponent'. I remember him coming to the set and taking us all out for dinner. He was very generous and sweet like that...When I met him again on 'Father Brown', he was very jovial, easy, and just so relaxed behind the camera. A natural performer and [it was] an education watching him act. I was lucky to work with him. I think he was more versatile than people think. I remember seeing him in the film version of 'The Deep Blue Sea'. He was excellent and his performance is very unapologetic. The dark side of him was wonderful to see, especially for someone so popular – I think that character was more of a risk for him to do than people would think of now."

In 1975, Kenny was the guest of honour at a Variety Club lunch held in the Lancaster ballroom of the Savoy celebrating his 40th year in show business. It was packed with the glitterati of the day, with many standing up to pay homage to him over the course of the afternoon. Kenny even got the opportunity to woo the crowd, singing a few lines from his favourite song 'When You're Smiling'. The Variety Club ceremony was such a major national event it was even transmitted on Thames Television under the title; 'A Little More, Please!'

That same year, Kenny starred with Nigel Davenport in the TV drama 'Goose with Pepper', playing the role of Brigadier Salt Lumley. Christopher Timothy, who acted with Kenny in the programme, recounts working with him: "Kenneth More was very much a part of my youth, a proper British film star, and in the 1970s I played a small part in a play for Anglia TV starring the great Kenneth More! He was a star alright, without being in the least bit starry! As well as a serious talent, he was so easy and enjoyable to work with. Charming, jolly, patient and very generous of himself. He was a true gent and a delight, I am glad I knew him, albeit briefly."

In the mid 1970s Anglia Television approached director Alvin Rakoff about making a television adaptation of 'In Praise of Love' (1976) by Terence Rattigan. It was based on the real-life relationship of actors Rex Harrison and Kay Kendall and the story of her terminal illness. Alvin Rakoff recalls its inception. "'In Praise of Love' came about as a play because of a discussion I had with Rattigan. He had told me of the Kay Kendall and Rex Harrison story and I said to Rattigan that he should write about that. He sort of ignored it. Some time later he wrote 'In Praise of Love', which was that story (originally entitled 'After Lydia'). When it came time to do it for television I directed it and cast Kenny in the lead alongside Claire Bloom. It was one of the best performances Kenny ever gave. Rattigan was very happy with it." 'In Praise of Love' aired to great acclaim, and upon reflection, it is probably his last, best screen work.

Kenny's godson, Michael Porter, a real gentleman, spent some time with me recollecting memories of his famous godfather. "I was at a school called Audley House, which was just outside of Chesterton. My mother (Pat Porter) had previously gone out with John Ringling, one of the Ringling brothers who founded one of the largest American circuses. John was over from the States one weekend and had come to stay with us in Woodstock. Kenny was there too. John arrived in this huge Mercedes with a chauffeur. He said to my father (Cyril Porter), who was Kenny's best friend, 'Why don't you and Kenny take the Mercedes and go and pick Michael up from school?'

"This huge car arrived on the driveway of the school and all the kids looked out of the window to see who it was, and to my amazement my father got out with Kenny!

"We all surrounded the car and then Kenny said to us 'who has a cricket bat and a ball? I'll give a pound to anyone who can catch it after I hit it into the sky!' He must have had sixty or seventy kids around him trying to catch the cricket ball and god knows what it cost him, but everyone got a pound!

"I can remember another occasion when he came to our home for the weekend with one of his best friends, Roger Moore. Whenever we went out with Kenny we would get stopped for an autograph, but having Roger Moore there too was something else. I remember we went down with them into the little supermarket in Woodstock and by the time we came out there was a crowd awaiting autographs! Kenny was always very good with people and was always happy to talk to them. It was all part of the deal of being a film star.

"He had quite simple tastes when it came to home cooking, very traditional English food. He wasn't fussy at all. He was very fond of cars. I remember he had a light blue 190SL Mercedes, which he was very fond of. He then had an MGB GT V8 and I remember it had these special-looking clocks on the dashboard. He always used to wear leather driving gloves too. He was always immaculately dressed. He took a lot of pride in his appearance. Very smart clothes, a crease in his trousers, but always casually dressed, lots of mock turtleneck jumpers, a tweed jacket. He was archetypically British like that. For supper out, always a shirt and tie. When he told stories you sometimes had to beg him to stop for your jaw was aching with laughter. I don't think I have ever laughed that way again the way I did when he was around.

I remember when I was a waiter at the Savoy Grill, around 1976, Kenny came in for lunch one day with Sterling Moss and Douglas Bader. It was quite something! He invited my father and me to the Garrick Club one day. He loved that place. They used to call him 'The Head Boy' there. He introduced my father to a gentleman, saying 'this is the man with the biggest c**k in London'. I was startled! As we went into dinner I asked my father, 'who was that man?' It was Justice Melford Stevenson! We sat in this huge dining room and you just sat next to whoever was there, and you met all sorts of people from high walks of life. To me, he was unbelievably kind and thoughtful. He would arrive at our home with cake and presents. As a godfather he gave me a beautiful Bulova Accutron watch, which he had engraved. He remembered how much I liked the one he wore. He also bought me some lovely cufflinks, which I still have. I miss him greatly, he was such fun."

'The Slipper and the Rose' (1976), directed by friend and fellow actor Bryan Forbes, saw Kenny in the role as Lord Chancellor, and singing yet again. It is hard not to think of this film without hearing the tones of the Sherman Brothers song 'Protocoligorically Correct', performed by Michael Hordern, Kenneth More, Peter Graves, and Tim Barrett. For once Kenny is attached to, what is considered by many to be, a hidden musical gem. Sadly, it does not get enough airplay compared to the Sherman Brothers songs for 'Mary Poppins'. Kenny's dance marching is also an endearing watch. He recalls a funny moment with Dame Edith Evans during filming:

"During this picture, we needed to film some scenes inside a large cathedral. No one would allow this until the Bishop of Southwark,

Mervyn Stockwood, gave his permission to film in his cathedral; I think he was a bit stage-struck. It was a very hot summer, and we were filming inside with candles burning, incense smoking and arc lights blazing away. Edith Evans was pretty old and she sat next to me. She was playing the Dowager Queen and I was the Lord Chamberlain. Michael Hordern was the King. Edith dozed in the heat. Whenever she woke up, she would say her one line whether she was on cue or not: 'I think that girl should go.'

She hadn't much to say, but she remembered it well. Whenever I saw her head nod, I rather naughtily nudged her. Edith would immediately perk up and say smartly and with perfect enunciation, 'I think that girl should go.'"

Further TV and film performances followed throughout the late 1970s but none had the magic of Kenny's earlier work. His final stage work would be as the Duke of Bristol, alongside Patricia Routledge as Maria Wislack, in Frederick Londsdale's 'On Approval' (1977) at the Vaudeville theatre.

The release of his final autobiography 'More or Less' (1978) was reported to have sold 100,000 copies almost immediately upon release. It received widespread critical and public praise and showed that Kenny's appeal had not diminished after four decades in the business, despite how times had changed. A successful paperback edition followed.

Sadly, Kenny's health started to deteriorate shortly afterwards. The doctors diagnosed him with a rare form of Parkinson's disease. Although he continued to work and appear in public for as long as he could, he announced his retirement from public life in 1980. His final role was that of Dr. Jarvis Lorry in a film adaptation of Charles Dickens' 'A Tale of Two Cities' (1980). It is a touching performance by Kenny, though sadly due to the illness he was suffering with his dialogue was dubbed in post production. The fact that he was able to complete filming despite being unwell shows you just how remarkable he was.

Michael Whitehall again: "He was the most generous man I think I have ever met in my life. He would tip everybody. He always had a bundle of pound notes in his back pocket. He wanted to pay for everything and was very generous with presents. Towards the end of his life he was going to be doing a film and I did a deal for him to do it. It wasn't a huge part, but it was a nice part. He was already slightly ill by then, but then he got very ill. He was very frail. It was very sad at the end. He didn't want people to see him either. He rang me up one day and said 'I feel terrible about this, but I am going to have to let you down. I don't think I can do that film. I'm really not well.' So, I rang the producer and he understood. A couple of weeks later I got a cheque from him for a sum of money. I looked at it and thought 'why has he sent me this cheque?' He had put a note in saying 'this is for you darling, the commission you would have had if I had done that film.'

"I obviously sent the cheque back and thanked him very much. That was very him and I must say that was a first and a last, for an actor to send you a commission for a part they couldn't do because they weren't well! He was amazing. He was probably my favourite actor of anyone I have ever had anything to do with. He was just unique...so kind... I was so fond of him."

In the twilight of his life, with the day-to-day support of Angela, he led a quiet life at home away from the media, preferring that the public and the industry remembered him as he once was. Some of their most contented moments together were sitting in the sun in their walled garden in Fulham, resting, reading and remembering so many wonderful memories.

Possibly, his last public communication was a letter he wrote and signed which was presented on screen by Angela on the occasion of Douglas Bader's 'This is Your Life', on 2nd March 1982. Kenny was by now too sick to attend. It read: 'My dear Douglas, You know very well why I can't be with you this evening. More the pity! But I'm sending my old lady along to represent me. She's been in love with you for years anyway! Your inspiration and courage is, quite rightly, a legend. It was with me all through the film and is with me still. "Up the R.A.F." Love from us both. Kenny.'

Kenneth More fought on until the very end with great bravery, passing away on 12th July 1982 at the age of 67 with Angela by his side. Subsequently Angela was to discover that Kenny had most likely been suffering with the rare degenerative neurological disorder known as Multiple System Atrophy, which would have explained why his condition deteriorated so rapidly. The tributes came flooding in almost immediately from all corners of the world.

On 5th September, Douglas Bader passed away from a heart attack, just months after Kenny.

Kenneth More's memorial was held at St Martin-in-the-Fields on 20th September 1982, which also marked his birthday. The service was packed with family and friends alike, among them: Lauren Bacall, Dame Anne Neagle and Lady Bader. A plaque was erected at St. Paul's Church Covent Garden, known more commonly as the Actor's Church.

It is almost 40 years since his passing, yet Kenny's performances have endured. Hopefully now his public profile will do the same.

Director Alvin Rakoff again: "Being, seeing and talking with Kenny was always a joy. The glass was always half full...he was a very positive man; he had a very warm attitude to life which was conveyed to anyone he was talking to, that's why I think he was so liked. He had this extraordinary affability which spread itself to everyone. I think he will be remembered for his smile."

The last words in Kenny's story have to come, of course, from the man himself. They remind me of how he should be remembered to this very day. At his best on-screen:

"In an upside down world, with all the rules being re-written as the game goes on and spectators invading the pitch, it is good to feel that some things and some people seem to stay just as they were."

8

"The book impressed me because it was about personal courage, and, as Churchill declared, courage is rightly esteemed the first of human qualities because it is the one which guarantees all others."
Kenneth More on 'The White Rabbit'

William Wyler's 'The Collector' (1965) starring Terence Stamp, Samantha Eggar and Mona Washbourne, started life very differently. A specially filmed prologue running for 35 minutes featured Kenny playing the part of Eggar's secret lover J.B.

Hollywood director Wyler was especially keen for Kenny to be cast in the role. More was flattered and hoped this would turn around his acting career on the big screen following a dip in the casting of major roles. Having seen the rushes, Kenny considered it one of his best performances; unfortunately, in post-production it was decided the prologue did not work with the rest of the film in the way Wyler hoped. More's entire role ended up on the cutting room floor. Angela More remembers: "Kenny just took it in his stride, but he knew the film business would assume he had given a bad performance and that was the real reason why his role was dropped. Show business can be so cutting. It felt like another nail in his career as a leading man. Thank god things were about to change, as only a few years later came 'The Forsyte Saga' and that put his star higher than it had ever been before."

After completing filming of 'The Forsyte Saga', Kenny was holidaying in Jamaica where he read a book, 'The White Rabbit'. It was the true story of Wing-Commander Yeo-Thomas who became a resistance hero in France during the Second World War and was subsequently caught and tortured by the Nazis. In his final autobiography, 'More or Less', Kenny recounts how taken he was with Yeo-Thomas's courage at the hands of his captors, much in the way he had been with Douglas

Bader's determination. When Kenny returned to England after learning of the success of 'The Forsyte Saga', he went to see David Attenborough, who was then in charge of Features at the BBC. He told him how much he would like to play the part. But there were problems. Attenborough discovered that the rights were held by Hal Chester. He would not give permission for the series in case he decided to make a film of the book himself, and so the idea seemed a non-starter. However, the BBC was able to overcome this obstacle by making only one transmission, never repeating it or selling that programme elsewhere.

The 'The White Rabbit' became a four-part series for the BBC in 1967. It was thought by many to be one of Kenny's best performances, equally on par with his role as Bader, if not superseding it. Kenny considered it his hardest physical role, and it was also the darkest drama he had ever appeared in. Reported to have cost £50,000 to produce, this was a dark retelling of a battle of wits between the interrogator and the interrogated, featuring gruelling torture scenes. A big departure from how audiences had witnessed him before. It was extremely well received. Sadly, due to the conditions of the one-off airing the tapes were destroyed. Kenny was very sad at this decision, but knew this would be the case when going into production.

I always thought Kenny had one strong dramatic role left to deliver following 'The Forsyte Saga', something that stretched him and showed an audience how much he still had to offer in serious, dramatic roles. Although starring roles in such dramas as 'In Praise of Love' (1976) and 'An Englishman's Castle' (1978) gave him later opportunities,

I still believe 'The White Rabbit' would have done much more to showcase his wider talents. Hope springs eternal it may one day resurface.

CONCLUSION

9

"A star...a man of the people, an actor of his time.
Ultimately, he should be remembered for his
immense talent. His incredible, natural skill at
making it all look so effortless. This should not be
mistaken for playing oneself. That is the artistry of
exceptional acting performance."
The Author

Along this journey I have been fortunate enough to discover who the real Kenneth More was. How he was distantly related to Sir Thomas More, Henry VIII's Lord Chancellor. His multifaceted personality. His zest for life and sense of fun. How socially he was always up for a lark, the life and soul of the party, but at home he was quiet and thoughtful, preferring to shut the world out. His keen desire for a quiet Christmas, but a lively New Year's Eve. Incredibly practical, a retentive eye. Worrying was a waste of time; it was better spent trying to tackle a problem than agonising over it. Things always sorted themselves out in the end. He was very professional at work, always the first at a rehearsal. However, not a perfectionist unless he felt really stirred by something. Then there was his dislike of bad manners, unpunctuality, and untidiness. His natural desire to fight injustice where he found it, always supporting the underdog. His great moral and physical courage in those last years of illness. His patriotism. He was quintessentially English.

His passion for his profession: "*I love acting, and that is sufficient recompense for me. I am not the sort of man who needs a Rolls or a Yacht. I had a Rolls once and got that out of my system...so long as I can have my poached egg on toast and 'three up and two down', I'll be happy, especially if there is a view of traffic going by...*"

His generosity: "*I enjoy entertaining my friends...I like to pick up the bill when it is presented, not for any question of showing off, but to prevent somebody feeling embarrassed because he may not be able to afford even his share of it...*"

His love of the Garrick club: "*If I only had enough money left in the world to pay the club subscription and nothing else, I would pay it."* His impeccable manners and incredible generosity. His charitable work; the mental health of ex-servicemen and women, The Variety Club for children...

A star...a man of the people...an actor of his time. Ultimately, he should be remembered for his immense talent. His incredible, natural skill at making it all look so effortless. This should not be mistaken for playing oneself. That is the artistry of an exceptional performance.

I have learned a great deal from researching his life. It came at precisely the right moment in my life, and has allowed me to look at many things with a fresh pair of eyes. Then there are the wonderful people I have met along the way and the opportunities it has provided me. I started this story by recalling how I had never known my own grandfather and the feeling of incapacity that I had experienced at not being able to have his name remembered properly. Up until now I had always felt there was something missing in my life because of it. Having been awarded the opportunity to do just so for my childhood hero has gone a long way to filling that gap. Perhaps most of all I have learned to live in the moment more, not to take things too seriously, to share the good times with others along the way, and to stay true to my principles. Maybe that is the sort of grandfatherly advice I would have been given, and perhaps now, I have finally received. For that reason alone, I am grateful for this experience.

To conclude this book, I wanted to find one fine and light-hearted example that epitomised Kenny's love of life, reflecting a man who never squandered the time he was given on this earth. There were so many to choose from, it was hard to select just one, so I have chosen two, and for the first Kenny will share it with you in his own words. It took place whilst filming 'Some People' in 1962.

"*While making this film, I had a call from Lady Astor, the daughter of Earl Haig, a charming woman who did a great deal of work for charity...she invited us to a private dinner party to meet the Queen, in her town house near Lowndes Square. She swore me to secrecy, because if news leaked out to the Press that I was to be a guest, the whole point of a private evening would be lost. I explained to James Archibald (the producer on 'Some People') that I had to go to London for some unexpected business and I arranged to take a day away from filming...I arrived at Lady Astor's house; it was clear that the host and hostess were both concerned about me because I am an extrovert. They were afraid that after a few drinks I might embarrass them, so they warned me: 'For God's sake, Kenny, remember, if you don't behave tonight you will be in the Tower...'*

That was said jokingly of course, but I noted the hint of apprehension behind the remark.

The Queen arrived with her lady-in-waiting, and the atmosphere before dinner was rather formal with everyone on edge and each of us waiting for someone else to begin the conversation. I had been presented to the Queen at first nights and at several Royal Film Performances, but this was quite a different thing. She knew who I was, and, of course, I knew who she was, but that was about it. After dinner, when I had been able to drink a little, I thought, to hell with this, I can't stifle myself anymore. I must be who I am. The result was that this turned out to be one of the most delightful evenings I have ever spent in my life.

I knew from others that the Queen could become quiet if she did not like someone, but if she is interested and being entertained, then she can relax completely. She stayed until half past one in the morning, and I sat on the floor swapping stories with her. Both of us spend a lot of time on our feet in our respective careers, and I wondered whether she had any bunions. She took her shoes off and showed me that she hadn't! It was a marvellous and relaxed evening, but afterwards I knew my host and hostess breathed a sigh of relief because I could either have gone too far or not far enough. As it happened, I had been as a frank and as unembarrassed as I could be, and the result had been successful."

The second story is told by Angela More:

"I remember one night towards the end of October in the late sixties, Kenny was invited to a very formal evening to commemorate Trafalgar Day. A dinner was to take place on board Nelson's flagship, HMS *Victory* in Portsmouth Dockyard. Kenny was excited, as Nelson had been one of his childhood heroes. He looked so smart in his tuxedo. I had especially bought him diamond button studs and matching cufflinks for the event. He left the house looking like a child with the anticipation of Christmas Day ahead of him.

It was early in the morning when I awoke wondering where he was. Moments later there was an almighty crash downstairs and in he came stumbling through the front door. He looked like he had been in the wars; his hair was discombobulated, his suit full of scuffs and his shirt fully open with the studs and cufflinks all missing. 'What on earth happened?' I asked him in a fright.

'I'm so sorry darling, it went on rather a long time and we all got a bit too excited. Last thing I remember was playing leapfrog over one of the guests on the top deck. The buttons and cufflinks must have fallen through the deck when I crash landed. Please forgive me!' He exclaimed.

'I thought it was a serious and formal reception you were going to?' I replied. 'It was!' he said. That says it all really!"

ACKNOWLEDGMENTS

This book could not have been written without the extensive help, support and contribution of Angela More. For her generosity and patience with my endless questions. Angela has been the very backbone of this journey.

Kenneth More's daughters, Jane More and Sarah More, both have been so very gracious with their involvement, time and support, allowing me into their lives and opening up about their father.

Heartfelt appreciation to the following contributors who shared their experiences of working with Kenneth More:

Wendy Craig, Vivyan Ellacott,
Susan Hampshire, Martin Jarvis,
Ronald Pickup, Michael Porter,
Christopher Timothy, Michael Whitehall.

Special gratitude to contributor Alvin Rakoff. I was fortune enough to spend considerable time recounting his memories of directing Kenneth More in multiple projects.

To Amanda Williams, who kindly gave me permission to use a photograph for the front cover from the collection of her grandfather, cameraman, Douglas J. Williams.

Additional thanks to those who have been of great
support:

Patrick Barlow, Ian Devlin,
Sarah Epton, Nicholas Horne,
Mariella Johnson, Michael Juliano,
Rob Kraitt, Rebecca Lake,
Peter Lee, Anthony Mestriner,
Caroline Taggart

ILLUSTRATIONS

SELECT BIBLIOGRAPHY AND NOTES

The source material for 'More, Please' is drawn in large part from Kenneth More's autobiography, 'More or Less' (1978), following the rights having reverted to the Kenneth More estate in 2019. Additional reference material includes letters and notes (handwritten and typescript), film and theatre press materials from the Kenneth More estate and Kenneth More Theatre, personal testimonials from family and friends (oral and typescript), and many programmes from the viewing library at the British Film Institute. Apart from 'Happy Go Lucky' (Robert Hale, 1959) and 'Kindly Leave The Stage' (Michael Joseph, 1965), both by Kenneth More, the most useful primary and secondary works consulted are listed below.

Afternoon Plus: TV interview (Thames Television, 1978)
A Little More Please: TV Variety Club lunch tribute (Thames Television, 1975)
Everybody's: film-related print feature (June 21st, 1956)
Ilford Recorder: Kenneth More Theatre closure article (29 August 2019)
Illustrated London News: film-related print feature (April 19th, 1969)
John Bull magazine: film-related print feature (April 16th, 1955)
Late Night Line-Up: TV interview (BBC, July 4th, 1967)
Ken Windsor: radio interview (Ken Windsor, 1970)

Look and Learn magazine: film-related print feature (December 4th, 1965)

Looks Familiar: TV guest appearance (Thames Television, April 3rd, 1980)

Motion Picture Herald trade newspaper annual polls for most popular stars at the box office (1954-1962)

Over the Footlights: Kenneth More biography (Vivyan Ellacott, 2011)

Photoplay magazine: print obituary (September 1982)

Picturegoer magazine: film-related print features
- - (June 13th, 1953)
- - (August 22nd, 1953)
- - (April 10th, 1954)
- - (April 24th, 1954)
- - (February 26th, 1955)
- - (January 28th, 1956)
- - (January 5th, 1957)
- - (June 8th, 1957)
- - (June 28th, 1958)
- - (July 26th, 1958)
- - (December 6th, 1958)

Picture Show supplement: Fans Star Library: Kenneth More special (No. 44, 1960)

Picture Show magazine: film-related print features
- - (May 1st, 1954)
- - (June 15th, 1957)
- - (October 11th, 1958)
- - (December 27th, 1958)
- - (November 21st, 1959)

Radio Times magazine: television print features
- - (November 29th, 1962)
- - (September 16th, 1967)
- - (April 16th, 1970)
- - (July 31st, 1971)
- - (June 3rd, 1978)

Talking Pictures: TV profile (BBC, 2015)

The Times: print feature on memorial mass (September 21st, 1982)

This Is Your Life: TV profile of Douglas Bader (Thames Television, March 31st, 1982)

Television Today: film related print feature (March 17th, 1966)

TV Times magazine: television-related print features
- - (September 21st, 1974)
- - (August 19th, 1975)

Notes:

It is important to recognise that I have discovered some inconsistencies, with names, dates, and times referenced by Kenneth More when retelling his life story in interviews he gave. To that end I have used 'More, Please', his final autobiography, as the basis on which to chronicle his story.

Further reading on the life of Kenneth More can be found at his official website run on behalf of his estate: KennethMore.com

Printed in Great Britain
by Amazon